American Enterprise Institute for Public Policy Research

Constitutional Controversies

Edited by
Robert A. Goldwin,
William A. Schambra, Art Kaufman

William B. Allen
Walter Berns
Henry O. Brandon
Dick Cheney
Lloyd N. Cutler
John Charles Daly
Drew S. Days III
Lee H. Hamilton
Benjamin L. Hooks
Charles McC. Mathias, Jr.

Abner Mikva
James C. Miller III
Norman Ornstein
Leon E. Panetta
Wm. Bradford Reynolds
Brent Scowcroft
Laurence H. Silberman
Laurence Tribe
J. Clifford Wallace
James Q. Wilson

Constitutional Controversies

**American Enterprise Institute
for Public Policy Research**

A DECADE OF STUDY OF THE CONSTITUTION

How Democratic Is the Constitution?

Robert A. Goldwin and William A. Schambra, editors

How Capitalistic Is the Constitution?

Robert A. Goldwin and William A. Schambra, editors

How Does the Constitution Secure Rights?

Robert A. Goldwin and William A. Schambra, editors

Separation of Powers: Does It Still Work?

Robert A. Goldwin and Art Kaufman, editors

How Federal Is the Constitution?

Robert A. Goldwin and William A. Schambra, editors

Selected Writings and Speeches of Alexander Hamilton

Morton J. Frisch, editor

Constitutional Controversies

Edited by
Robert A. Goldwin,
William A. Schambra, Art Kaufman

William B. Allen	Abner Mikva
Walter Berns	James C. Miller III
Henry O. Brandon	Norman Ornstein
Dick Cheney	Leon E. Panetta
Lloyd N. Cutler	Wm. Bradford Reynolds
John Charles Daly	Brent Scowcroft
Drew S. Days III	Laurence H. Silberman
Lee H. Hamilton	Laurence Tribe
Benjamin L. Hooks	J. Clifford Wallace
Charles McC. Mathias, Jr.	James Q. Wilson

American Enterprise Institute for Public Policy Research
Washington, D.C.

The AEI Project, "A Decade of Study of the Constitution," of which publication of this anthology is one activity, has been funded in part by a grant from the National Endowment for the Humanities.

Distributed by arrangement with

UPA, Inc.
4720 Boston Way   3 Henrietta Street
Lanham, MD 20706   London WC2E 8LU England

Library of Congress Cataloging-in-Publication Data

Constitutional controversies / Robert A. Goldwin, William A. Schambra,
Art Kaufman, editors.
    p.   cm.
  ISBN 0-8447-2272-3 (alk. paper). ISBN 0-8447-2271-5 (pbk. : alk.
paper)
  1. United States—Constitutional law.   I. Goldwin, Robert A.,
1922–   . II. Schambra, William A.   III. Kaufman, Art.
KF4550.A2C66   1987
342.73'029—dc19
[347.30229]   87-16462
                                                             CIP

SYM-87A   Printed in the United States of America

The American Enterprise Institute separately published *President vs. Congress* in 1981, *War Powers and the Constitution* in 1984, and *Affirmative Action and the Constitution* in 1987.

Contents

Preface

"At the first sound of a new argument over the United States Constitution and its interpretation, the hearts of Americans leap with a fearful joy. The blood stirs powerfully in their veins and a new lustre brightens their eyes." So wrote the London *Economist* in 1952. The occasion was the controversy provoked by President Truman's seizure of the steel mills during the Korean War, but the observation could apply just as well to any epoch of our history and is certainly no less true today. No matter how mundane or momentous the issue, Americans always seem compelled by the system itself to discover and to debate its constitutional dimensions.

Recognizing this phenomenon, the American Enterprise Institute has, over the past ten years, devoted a number of Public Policy Forums, or videotaped panel discussions, to the Constitution and its bearing on current public policy questions. The texts of the five discussions printed herein give some idea of the range and depth of our Founding document's involvement with today's issues. Among the questions addressed by these panels, which include prominent public officials, scholars, and journalists, are:

• Does the separation of powers still guard our liberty by preventing "the accumulation of all powers into the same hands," as the Founders intended? Or has it made government weak and confused by producing deadlock between the president and Congress?

• Does the War Powers Resolution of 1973 unconstitutionally restrict the president as commander in chief? Or is it a legitimate use of Congress's constitutional powers to make and execute foreign policy?

• Is the current budget process—as reorganized most recently in the Congressional Budget and Impounding Control Act of 1974—adequate for the development of sound federal budgets? Or do some of today's budget deficit problems point to the need for dramatic structural and even constitutional changes in the process?

• Are race-conscious remedies necessary to increase minority group opportunities in employment and admissions to colleges and professional schools? Or are such preferences unconstitutional reverse discrimination?

• When we interpret the Constitution today, should we do so in light of the intentions of the framers of the document? Or do we thereby make it a static document instead of "a living Constitution" devoted to achieving social progress?

This is a book of controversies, lively and spirited, representing a full range of viewpoints on the issues. Nonetheless, in all of the disagreements there is an underlying consensus that our Founding document is an invaluable source of guidance to Americans as we address the issues of our day.

We see, therefore, the value of what the late Martin Diamond described as the "constitutionalization" of our politics: "Political forces align themselves as rival interpretations of an agreed upon constitutional regime, rather than one side defending and the other attacking the regime itself." Because our political controversies thus tend to assume the form of disputes over the meaning and application of the Constitution, they tend to be more moderate and peaceful than those divisive issues that plague many nations today.

Another important consequence of the constitutionalization of our politics is that it "persistently keeps the Constitution before our eyes." Even as we address the most urgent and contentious of our political problems, we are necessarily reminded of the Founding principles upon which we are all agreed and from which our liberty and prosperity flow.

These panel discussions, accordingly, demonstrate that our Constitution is observed and celebrated not only on the occasion of its anniversaries—of which this year we observe the two hundredth—but every day in the give-and-take of American politics as well.

ROBERT A. GOLDWIN
WILLIAM A. SCHAMBRA
ART KAUFMAN

Participants

President vs. Congress: Does the Separation of Powers Still Work?

HENRY O. BRANDON, Washington bureau chief, London *Sunday Times*

LLOYD N. CUTLER, counsel to President Carter

LAURENCE H. SILBERMAN, circuit judge, U.S. Circuit Court of Appeals for the District of Columbia, former deputy attorney general, ambassador to Yugoslavia, and under secretary of labor

JAMES Q. WILSON, Collins Professor of Management, University of California, Los Angeles

JOHN CHARLES DALY, former ABC News chief, moderator

Discussion held on November 25, 1980

War Powers and the Constitution

DICK CHENEY, U.S. representative (Republican, Wyoming), chairman of the House Republican Policy Committee, and former White House chief of staff in the Ford administration

LEE H. HAMILTON, U.S. representative (Democrat, Indiana) and member of the House Foreign Affairs Committee and of the Permanent Select Committee on Intelligence

CHARLES McC. MATHIAS, JR., former U.S. senator (Republican, Maryland), member of the Senate Foreign Relations Committee, and second ranking member of the Senate Judiciary Committee

BRENT SCOWCROFT, lieutenant general-retired, U.S. Air Force, former chairman of President Reagan's Commission on Strategic Forces, and former national security adviser to President Ford

JOHN CHARLES DALY, former ABC News chief, moderator

Discussion held on December 6, 1983

The Constitution and the Budget Process

DICK CHENEY, U.S. representative (Republican, Wyoming), chairman of the House Republican Policy Committee, and former White House chief of staff in the Ford administration

JAMES C. MILLER III, director of the Office of Management and Budget and former chairman of the Federal Trade Commission

NORMAN ORNSTEIN, resident scholar of the American Enterprise Institute and a visiting professor of political science at Johns Hopkins University

LEON E. PANETTA, U.S. representative (Democrat, California), member of House Budget Committee, and former chairman of the Budget Committee's Task Force on Reconciliation

JOHN CHARLES DALY, former ABC News chief, moderator

Discussion held on December 3, 1985

Affirmative Action and the Constitution

WILLIAM B. ALLEN, professor of government, Department of Humanities and Social Sciences, Harvey Mudd College, and member of the California State Advisory Committee of the U.S. Commission on Civil Rights

DREW S. DAYS III, associate professor of law, Yale Law School, former assistant attorney general in charge of the Civil Rights division, and former assistant counsel to the NAACP Legal Defense and Educational Fund

BENJAMIN L. HOOKS, executive director, National Association for the Advancement of Colored People (NAACP), and chairman, Leadership Conference on Civil Rights

WM. BRADFORD REYNOLDS, assistant attorney general in charge of the Civil Rights Division and former assistant to the solicitor general of the United States

JOHN CHARLES DALY, former ABC News chief, moderator

Discussion held on May 21, 1985

How Should We Interpret the Constitution?

WALTER BERNS, John M. Olin University Professor at Georgetown University and adjunct scholar at the American Enterprise Institute

ABNER MIKVA, circuit judge, U.S. Court of Appeals for the District of Columbia, and former Democratic congressman from Illinois

LAURENCE TRIBE, Ralph Tyler Professor of Constitutional Law at Harvard University Law School

J. CLIFFORD WALLACE, circuit judge, U.S. Court of Appeals for the Ninth District, and former U.S. district judge for the Southern District of California

ROBERT A. GOLDWIN, resident scholar and director of Constitutional Studies of the American Enterprise Institute, moderator

Discussion held on September 17, 1986

1
President
vs.
Congress
Does the Separation
of Powers
Still Work?

Henry O. Brandon
Lloyd N. Cutler
John Charles Daly
Laurence H. Silberman
James Q. Wilson

J OHN CHARLES DALY, former ABC News chief and forum moderator: This public policy forum, part of a series presented by the American Enterprise Institute, is concerned with whether the historic separation of powers among the executive, legislative, and judicial branches of the government, enshrined in our Constitution, encourages stalemate and inefficiency and is potentially disastrous in this modern world. Our subject, "President vs. Congress: Does the Separation of Powers Still Work?"

Nearly 200 years ago, our Founding Fathers argued in the *Federalist Papers* that "the accumulation of all powers, legislative, executive, and judiciary, in the same hands, whether of one, a few, or many, and whether hereditary, self-appointed, or elective, may justly be pronounced the very definition of tyranny. . . . The preservation of liberty requires that the three great departments of power should be separate. . . ."

The underlying argument elsewhere in the *Federalist Papers* states, "The great security consists in giving to those who administer each department the necessary constitutional means and personal motives to resist encroachments of the others. Ambition must be made to counteract ambition."

Nearly 100 years ago, the Federalist concept was hotly challenged by one who would later be president of the United States, Woodrow Wilson. Wilson, denouncing the almost absolute power of the standing committees of the Congress and the overriding discipline of an external authority—the political party to which the majority of the Congress owed allegiance—called for cabinet government. He defined "cabinet government" as simply giving the heads of the executive departments, the members of the cabinet, seats in the Congress with the privilege of initiating legislation, and, he added acidly, "some part of the unbounded privileges now commanded by the standing committees."

3

In addition, Wilson argued that cabinet government necessarily involves the principle of ministerial responsibility. "According to their policy, and how it stands or falls," he said, "the ministers stand or fall. If defeated in both houses, he, the minister, would naturally resign, and resignation upon defeat is the essence of responsible government."

Still, in this parliamentary design, he, who was to be president, yet bent a knee to the principle of separation. He noted that it would be plainly at variance with republican principles to allow the president to choose whomever he pleases to the cabinet, thus making them ex officio members of the Congress, because it would give him the power to appoint members of Congress. "Rather," he said, "the highest order of responsible government could then be established in the United States only by laying upon the president the necessity of selecting his cabinet from among the number of representatives already chosen by the people, who would, of course, retain their seats."

Thus, in essence, was launched the debate in modern times on reform of our system of government toward the British parliamentary system, modifications of which are general in Western Europe and in Japan. The turmoil and frustrations of these past years, both in the domestic and foreign affairs areas, and urgent demands for more effective and efficient government, have renewed debate on the question of whether the separation of powers still works.

To lead us through this labyrinth, we have a highly expert panel: Mr. Henry O. Brandon, foreign correspondent, war correspondent, diplomatic correspondent, and now Washington bureau chief and associate editor of the London *Sunday Times*. Mr. Lloyd N. Cutler is a distinguished Washington attorney with broad experience on government and academic boards and commissions, capped by service in the White House as counsel to President Carter. Mr. Laurence H. Silberman, also a distinguished Washington attorney, has served as deputy attorney general of the United States, ambassador to Yugoslavia, undersecretary of labor, and was formerly a senior fellow at the American Enterprise Institute. Mr. Silberman is now an executive vice-president of the Crocker National Bank in San Francisco. Dr. James Q. Wilson, former director of the Joint Center for Urban Studies of MIT and Harvard, is a member of AEI's Council of Academic Advisers and is the Henry Lee Shattuck Professor of Government at Harvard.

Gentlemen, I will pose the same question to each of you: Is our traditional 200-year-old separation of powers an anachronism, made obsolete by the technology, mass, and speed of communications in modern society?

LLOYD N. CUTLER, counsel to President Carter: The separation of powers is an anachronism, and one in need of some revision. Along with Woodrow Wilson, I believe we do need to do a better job of forming a government in the parliamentary sense—one that can legislate and execute a balanced program for governing. With every succeeding administration, this need is becoming more acute.

The fault is not personal to any president or legislator. It is the structure of our Constitution and, in particular, the rigid separation between the legislative and the executive branches that prevent us from doing significantly better. It is time for all of us to start pondering and debating, in forums like this one, whether to correct this structural fault, and if so, how.

LAURENCE H. SILBERMAN, former deputy attorney general, ambassador to Yugoslavia, and undersecretary of labor: I disagree. I believe today, as people believed 200 years ago, that the separation of powers doctrine is an enormously important protection for American citizens. The separation of powers among the three branches of government makes it very difficult for the government to accrue power, and it is as desirable today as it was 200 years ago to make it difficult for the government to accrue power, because that is a potential threat to the well-being of citizens.

HENRY O. BRANDON, Washington bureau chief, London *Sunday Times*: I want to make it clear from the start that I do not mean to propose the imposition of the British monarchy or the British parliamentary system here. I am in favor of reforms of the present American political system. It is a system that is today the oldest and the least changed in the world. The office held today by the American president is far more like the office held by President Washington than that held by Queen Elizabeth II is like that held by George III.

The United States today is the leader of the free world. As such, it has to undertake some very major and important commitments. If the president cannot be sure that he can adhere to those commitments, it becomes very difficult for the United States to be recognized as a world leader.

JAMES Q. WILSON, Henry Lee Shattuck Professor of Government, Harvard University: To paraphrase Winston Churchill, the separation

5

of powers is a poor philosophy of government, except in comparison with all others. It has its defects. Those will probably come out in our discussion, perhaps notably with respect to the conduct of foreign affairs, but it has the virtues of those defects, as well. It facilitates scrutiny, sometimes at the expense of action; it protects the particular and the individual, sometimes at the expense of the general. But it has brought about the capacity to engage in great national commitments when important national emergencies arise, and above all it has permitted a union to be created out of great diversity by providing separate constitutional places on which individuals could focus their loyalties.

MR. DALY: Mr. Cutler, your article in *Foreign Affairs* in the closing months of 1980, entitled "To Form a Government," has brought debate on the separation of powers to center stage. You wrote particularly of the separation of powers between the legislative and executive branches. You said, "The separation of powers between these two branches, whatever its merits in 1793, has become a structure that almost guarantees stalemate today."

In very broad brush, you suggested that we should have candidates for president, vice-president, and Congress run as a team in all election districts; require, or allow, half of the cabinet to be members of the Congress; establish a six-year term for the president, the vice-president, and the members of the Senate and the House; and establish procedures for the president or Congress to be able when stalemates set in to call for general elections for the remainder of the current term, this election process to take no more than 120 days. Would you now develop these ideas?

MR. CUTLER: I did not advocate any of those constitutional revisions you enumerated—I simply tabulated them as ideas that had come to the fore. My central proposition is that we need to study and appreciate, more than we have, the costs of the separation of powers between the legislative and the executive branches. These costs need to be weighed alongside the admitted benefits. In 1980 and in the decades ahead, if not at some earlier time, we need a balanced program for governing, rather than a hodgepodge program for governing. Government has any number of important social and economic goals: controlling inflation, providing jobs, increasing productivity, ensuring social justice and social welfare, providing for our national defense, accepting America's role today as the guardian of the entire free world, protecting the environment. Not all of those goals can be pursued in full vigor at the same time, even in a country

6

as rich as this one, and the art of governing has become one of striking the proper balance among those goals. This would happen if a balanced program were presented to the electorate by candidates who, if elected, could then proceed to legislate and execute that balanced program.

My thesis is that today it is impossible for the elected president or the elected majority in either house or both houses of Congress to legislate and execute a balanced program. Given the structure of the presidency and the Congress and the many things that have happened to our party system—the growth of single-interest political groupings, the well-meant reforms of Congress—there is no way the policies adopted can be a balanced set of policies that anyone elected will endorse. The president does not endorse the package that emerges; it is not his program. It is not the program of a legislative majority. It is a program resulting from a series of individual, ad hoc majorities, each pursuing its own policy on each particular issue as it arises.

As a result, when failure comes, when the effort to pursue these various policies gets out of balance, we have no one to hold accountable. The president cannot fairly be blamed, because his program has not been adopted. The majority of Congress, or the minority, cannot fairly be blamed; the majority differs from one measure to another, and the minority does not have any particular program of its own.

This is a basic problem of American government, not shared by parliamentary governments, including those with writtten constitutions. Ironically, we helped to write many of those—notably the constitutions of Germany and Japan—in the postwar era. It may be that some of the deficiencies that have resulted—that is, the lack of power in any one official or in any group of elected officials to enact a balanced program and execute it—could be cured by nonconstitutional measures. Nevertheless, they are structural problems that every president elected in this century has had to endure and that every president, with the possible exception of FDR in the face of two great national crises that helped to bring us together, has been unable to solve.

MR. SILBERMAN: Given one axiom or one hypothesis, I would agree entirely with Mr. Cutler. If we could find the balanced program that we could all agree upon, he would be absolutely right. In fact, however, there is no such thing as a balanced program. There is one program, another program, and still another program.

Mr. Cutler cites in his article an example of an "excellent" piece of legislation, the SALT treaty, which all people would recognize was "balanced." Yet, a significant minority, perhaps a majority, in this country thought it was awful and thought the president behaved imprudently in negotiating it. He had been signaled at the very outset, when forty senators voted against the confirmation of his arms control negotiator, that he was going to have a very difficult time getting the SALT treaty through the Senate. Had he been more prudent, he might have come up with a different treaty and might have gotten it through.

We cannot accept the proposition that what President Carter thought was balanced—a treaty that was worked out through a bureaucratic clash between various executive branch agencies—was superior in any way to legislation or treaties that would come out of the process of the executive proposing and the Congress compromising and legislating. In other words, there is no validity to Mr. Cutler's assertion that some magic kind of balanced program will come forth from an executive or a president if you just leave him alone.

DR. WILSON: Mr. Cutler has a philosophy of governance that is at odds with what the framers of the Constitution embodied in that document. To Mr. Cutler good policy or good government is the product or the act of a single will. It is an act of management, of allocation, of balance. The framers, by contrast, thought that good policy could be recognized when it appeared, but to achieve it in the real world required a process of ambition counteracting ambition, leading thereby to the formation of coalitions—coalitions of partial, self-interested groups. They hoped the Constitution would lead these coalitions to emerge only on the principle of the common good.

This has not always happened, but it is a first approximation of their effort. The difficulty and magnitude of our problems are admittedly great, but no greater than the problems other presidents in past centuries have had to deal with, and intellectually it is unlikely that we can devise a program that corresponds to a theory of governance based on the act of a single will or intelligence. Politically, it is unlikely that we can devise institutions that could translate that will, if formulated, into a desirable result.

Consider Great Britain. With due respect to Mr. Brandon, I do not see that great steady hand, that even philosophy of governance, that striking for balances emerging from the parliamentary system. Great Britain has nationalized and denationalized industry at a dizzying rate. It has perhaps the worst labor-management relations of any western democracy. It has had extraordinary difficulties in deciding

8

whether it will remain part of the European Community. I have profound sympathies with Britain's difficulties, because we would have had as many; those difficulties do not suggest that, once the appropriate parliamentary devices are in place there is a will, which, when revealed, will produce altogether good effects.

MR. BRANDON: First of all, I want to take issue with those who have blamed President Carter for these constitutional difficulties. It is also often said that the problems that have arisen are all the aftermath of Vietnam and Watergate. Neither is the case. As a practical example, in 1962, President Kennedy asked Congress for a tax cut; he labored for months, but he could not get it. It happened that I saw Prime Minister Macmillan at the time, in London, and he said to me, "You mean to say that if the American president wants a tax cut, he can't get a tax cut?" I said, "Yes, that's the case." He said, "You know, if I need a tax cut, I can get it within a month."

If a president decides that a tax cut is the right thing for this country, but he cannot get a tax cut, how on earth can he do the best for his country? How will Mr. Reagan be able to govern if he finds himself in a similar position? I do not know whether he will get his tax cut, and you cannot tell me whether he will get that tax cut.

It is very difficult for any government in this country to plan ahead. The country may want a long-term policy that stretches over two, three, or four years, particularly in the economic field, but if presidents cannot set and accomplish long-term goals, how can they govern?

MR. DALY: Franklin Roosevelt, Harry Truman—despite election year invective—Dwight Eisenhower, and Lyndon Johnson all managed to work effectively with Congress under varying conditions. There is no intent here to focus on President Carter, because we are really talking about the problems of the presidency with respect to the issue of separation of powers. Is it possible, however, that policy failure and stalemate, as we have identified it in our times, depend to a high degree on the incumbent in the White House?

MR. SILBERMAN: Of course. I hestiated to take up Mr. Cutler's example of President Carter's governance during the last four years, because the election is over and we should not be partisan anymore. I do believe, however, that President Carter brought a good part of his problems upon himself.

MR. CUTLER: I just hope we can have a repeat of this forum three and a half years from now, or perhaps earlier. [Laughter.]

MR. SILBERMAN: You have a guarantee. Incidentally, President Reagan's proposal for a tax cut is a balanced program. You will accept that, won't you? [Laughter.]

MR. CUTLER: I would like to see President Reagan and the elected majority—although unfortunately one does not exist—have the opportunity to carry out the Reagan programs, or the Republican platform programs.

MR. SILBERMAN: I understand your point. President Carter, however, governed very much in the philosophy of Lloyd Cutler's article. He took each problem by itself, like an ad hoc engineering problem, and felt there was a "right" solution, or to use Mr. Cutler's word, a "balanced" solution. He would arrive at this solution and spring it on the Congress, and then watch with astonishment when the Congress either rejected it, chewed it up by amendment, or ignored it.

The fact is that we want something more from a president than an intellectual will or the ability to promulgate messages. We want a savvy politician who can form consensus and who also comes to the presidency with some kind of coherent notion of what he wants to do with the presidency. After all, that is all he has, the presidency. If anyone goes back and looks at Jimmy Carter's campaign promises, despite some of the allusions in Lloyd Cutler's article, it will be very difficult to find that coherent program. He came to office without a clear idea about doing anything except reorganizing the government and moving boxes around and theoretically creating fewer agencies, and he ended up creating more. Because he had no coherent idea of what he wanted to do and because he disdained the political process—the process by which you build consensus—it was inevitable that he would fail. Finding solace for that failure in the structure of the Constitution seems to me to be whistling in the dark.

MR. CUTLER: If we are going to get political, I am surprised, Mr. Silberman, that as a veteran of an administration of one president who was unable to complete his term, the only one who resigned in history, and another president who was unable to win an election, you would make remarks of that kind. The issue is whether anyone's program or any majority's program can be adopted. Is there anyone you know who served in the Ford or the Nixon administration who would totally endorse the programs that were followed during his administration? I submit that you will not find anyone. President Ford, again and again, was ready to criticize the Democratic Congress that did not allow him to carry out his programs.

One of the oddest things, one that helps to prove my point, is that we have a system not only in which the presidency and the majority in the Congress have been held by opposite parties for half of the last eight administrations—and this is also true for the new administration—but even when they are held by the same party, it does not seem to make any difference.

The opponents of SALT II had no balanced program of their own for governing. They might have had a way to go about controlling the arms race that they thought was best, but they had no solution as to how that was to be balanced with the other problems of the budget and unemployment and social justice and social security. No one is prepared to endorse the outcome of what our combined mélange of legislators and president comes up with. Essentially, it goes back, as I mention in my article, to old Joe Jacobs, the fight manager, who said, "It's every man for theirself."

As discussed in a recent AEI book, *Presidents and Prime Ministers*, when we speak of how the president ought to be able to manage the government, there is no one government to manage. There is a series of subgovernments pursuing single interests of one kind or another, and a new majority has to be formed on every single issue.

I would like to come back to Dr. Wilson's point that my thesis is at odds with that of the framers. I would agree with that, because the framers did not want a government that could manage our lives and manage all the problems we face in the world. If we believe that government should do the very least possible, not only in domestic affairs but in foreign affairs as well, the framers had a very good system for doing that.

I am not speaking of the act of a single will. I am not urging more power for the president and less power for the Congress. What I am urging is that the president and the elected majority in the Congress, in one way or another, be made to share the same political fate and take joint responsibility for forming a balanced program, carrying it out, and living or dying politically by the results. That is the central thesis.

How to accomplish that is a very, very difficult proposition, I admit. Unless it is accomplished, however, we will have stalemate and a continued mélange of policies that no elected official will endorse. This is an unsatisfactory method of governing ourselves in

11

this century, especially with our need to react promptly to new events and crises all over the world that are no longer within the reach of American military power.

DR. WILSON: I grant some force to your argument with respect to the conduct of foreign affairs, but in general it does not correspond to what the American people expect. They do not wish to have an opportunity to vote yes or no on a party's cohesive performance in office, in which it takes responsibility for the policies that have been put in place, because the American public does not exist as a public. It is a collection of separate publics that have discovered, or would readily admit if it were pointed out, that if they have to vote yes or no on a comprehensive set of policies, they cannot do so. They are torn with too many internal contradictions.

During the last 200 years, the people more or less successfully have modified policies by taking up the various constitutional opportunities presented to them—off-term elections for the House, six-year terms for the Senate, presidential elections, the congressional oversight process, the lobbying process, campaign contributions—as a way of giving expression to particular preferences, which the unlucky folk in Washington must cope with and try to put together into a coalition around each issue. This creates great difficulties for those who govern, difficulties so great that many persons, especially those associated with activist presidents, have regularly published books about "the deadlock of democracy." Whenever the deadlock is broken, however, as they allege it has been in recent years, they then write about the imperial presidency. That does not seem to be desirable, either. I agree that an imperial presidency is a mistake, but we have not had an imperial presidency, with perhaps a few exceptions.

The deadlock of democracy is not a deadlock at all; in the 1930s, the 1960s, and the 1970s, our system produced an extraordinary outpouring of legislative innovation because certain ideas were sufficiently coherent to permit change to occur.

The people are unwilling to vote simply yes or no in a national referendum about the record of a party because the people are too various. They want these diverse opportunities to peck and chip and constrain in order to moderate policy. If we compare American policy with that of most parliamentary democracies, its leading characteristic is its moderation. There are many policies I do not approve of and regularly call immoderate. Taken as a whole, however, we tend to temper the enthusiasm of temporary majorities by the need constantly to reformulate that majority.

12

MR. DALY: Mr. Brandon, to get to the possibility, which Mr. Cutler raised himself, that the reforms—if reform is needed—may be achieved without constitutional change, you have expressed approval of Senator Fulbright's argument that the method of selecting the American president reinforces the belief held around the world that our society is doomed by its internal contradictions. Senator Fulbright's major reform proposal is for the legislature to select the executive from among its own members.

Senator Moynihan and Representative Reuss, two congressional Democractic leaders, espoused putting members of Congress in the cabinet, which is something Mr. Cutler put out for debate and discussion. For the executive branch to become part of the legislative function would require a constitutional amendment. It has been suggested, however, that if they were unpaid members of the cabinet, with no specific portfolio, members of the Congress could be in the cabinet without any violation of the Constitution.

Do you see in these proposals any cure for what you consider our problems of conflict between the powers of the two relatively great branches of government?

MR. BRANDON: If there were a cure, it would create an imbalance. So, again, we have to assume that whatever reforms are introduced will improve the situation, but they will not solve it.

I have not actually endorsed Senator Fulbright's ideas. I would like to see, for the beginning at least, reforms introduced that can be achieved without constitutional amendments. If the leaders of the House and the Senate were brought into the policy-making process at a very early stage and made participants, that in itself would give the government's policy, and the impression that the policy-making creates for the public or for the world, a much greater stability and predictability.

I do not want to defend the parliamentary system, because that system would not work in this country. Nevertheless—I am so tempted by Dr. Wilson's needles—the British government accepted membership in the European Community and, although there has been plenty of opposition to it, it is still a member of the European Community. The British government signed a treaty and then acted on it. The American president signed, say, the SALT treaty, but cannot act on it. Unless the word of a president can be relied on and can be reinforced by the support of the principal leaders in Congress, it will be very difficult for the United States to carry out the kind of world leadership that everybody expects from it today.

13

MR. SILBERMAN: Mr. Cutler accurately stated the fundamental question, which lies at the heart of this issue. If we want government, all of government, to have greater power, then his suggestion makes sense. It is quite clear that if we move toward fusing aspects of the executive and legislative branches, as he wishes, we would create greater power for the government, as a whole. This is fundamental to the separation of powers. The American democracy, unique in the world, makes it very difficult for government to accrue power. The only way the government can accrue power, at least theoretically under our Constitution, is by legislation, by treaty, or by constitutional amendment.

Now, let us put judicial imperialism aside for a moment. It is a problem I talk about a lot, but it is not really the focus of this discussion. I would note, parenthetically, that Mr. Cutler calls for a constitutional convention on separation of powers; and although I totally disagree with him on his concern about the executive and the legislature, I agree that such a convention would be a good thing, because the judiciary has behaved in imperial fashion. Going back to my point, however, the American democracy was set up with the deliberate intention of making it very difficult for the government to accrue power. Government cannot get power without a consensus in the United States. Mr. Cutler thinks government ought to be able to get the power with a bare majority of some group, but I think the founders were right that the thing to worry about is governmental power, for the most part. Therefore, we should make it difficult for the government to accrue power.

The one area in which Mr. Cutler argues most strongly is in foreign affairs. He says the government—and by the government he means the executive branch—at least ought to be able to move more rapidly and without the constant trouble that a treaty ratification process causes. I go back to the point I made earlier on the SALT treaty, which is his major foreign policy example. If President Carter had negotiated a SALT treaty that he knew would command a consensus in the country and a majority of the Senate, he could have had it ratified. Instead, he chose to negotiate what he perceived to be a balanced program—that is to say, one that sprang from his mental processes and that the Senate should have taken because it was "right." That is just not politics; that is not American democracy.

MR. CUTLER: When you say the president had a choice between negotiating a SALT treaty that a majority of the Congress would support and the one he did negotiate, you are assuming that Mr. Brezhnev would sign whatever Mr. Carter proposed. I leave that

14

aside. I also leave aside that the SALT treaty was 85 percent—Mr. Reagan said, in this campaign, 90 percent—negotiated by Secretary Kissinger and President Ford.

MR. SILBERMAN: It was the other 10 percent that was obnoxious. [Laughter.]

MR. CUTLER: It was the 10 percent that Ford could have finished in 1976. He did not because he feared the Reagan attack in the convention. That is the fact of the matter.

But let's go on to something that everybody in this audience would agree on, and that is the budget. If there is any critical element to running a government or running an economy, it is a budget. We are the only democracy in the world, that I know of, in which the legislature is able to enact an aggregate budget and appropriations greater than the amount proposed by the leader of the government. We consistently have a budget with a higher deficit than the president wants, than the majority leaders want, than every member of Congress wants, because we cannot get together on a single budget.

The result of the mélange of interests that has been described makes us essentially ungovernable. We cannot have a budget—the central feature of modern government and of a modern economy today—for which either the elected president or any of the 535 elected members of the Congress will take responsibility. They all want a lower budget, but with more for their programs and less for somebody else's programs. That is not a government and that is not a responsible way of conducting ourselves in this latter half of the twentieth century.

MR. BRANDON: It comes down to the simple fact that there has to be someone who can define and determine the national interest. A body like Congress, in its composition today—not as it was about 100 years ago—cannot do that. It cannot formulate, for instance, a foreign policy. It cannot formulate a budget. A nation must have someone it can trust, and after all the president is elected by the people and has a vast variety of counselors. Assume that he can make mistakes, but maybe his mistakes, in the end, are less perilous than having no policy or having a hodgepodge of policies.

DR. WILSON: I wish we would not agree so readily that America has a foreign policy that is a hodgepodge. I disagree with many elements of it and certain tendencies of it, but we are speaking now of a country that won World War II, that put in place European recon-

15

struction, that rearmed the West, that created the NATO alliance, that gave aid to Greece and Turkey, that established a ring of alliances that gave some hope to democratic regimes in all parts of the world, and that fought Communist interventionism when it was not in our material interests to do so. Although we have surely made mistakes in the pursuit of all these objectives, that is not such bad policy. Would a stronger president have been a better one? Did General de Gaulle have a better policy when he was president of France, with certainly all the power he could have wished?

With respect to the budget, I agree that the budget cycle, which Mr. Cutler accurately describes, proves conclusively that the public interest differs from the summation of private wants (something that my colleagues in political science like to deny, but this fact establishes it). The question is, How do we deal with that? I am not sure it is by having a stronger president who can say, "This is my budget, take it or leave it." President Johnson did this during the Vietnam war and decided to print money to finance the deficit.

Perhaps we must have a sharper restriction on the budget. Though we have not mentioned it so far, if constitutional revision is to occur, perhaps we should consider a budget limitation linked to gross national product and public expenditures.

MR. DALY: We can all agree that the proposals Mr. Cutler put up for debate—and I stress "that he put up for debate"—would require constitutional change. Let us examine further the changes that might work but do not require amendment of the Constitution. Senate Republican leader Howard Baker, for instance, would like to see an official liaison presidential office on Capitol Hill and the appearance by the members of the cabinet before one or both houses of Congress at regular intervals to answer questions about executive policy. This proposal in years past has been generally endorsed by both President Carter and Vice President Mondale. Could that be a way to get consensus on a presidential program and, ultimately, its passage?

MR. CUTLER: All of these proposals are improvements, but they fall short of reaching the heart of the problem, which is shared political fates and responsibility for the majority of the legislature and the president. We need a way of doing that. In this election, of course, it is true that some of the Democratic senators shared the same political fate as the president. Nevertheless, it remains a fact that the president was defeated by some 6 million or 7 million votes, and a Democratic House was elected by a comfortable majority.

16

MR. SILBERMAN: Yes, but an important point to keep in mind is that a majority of people who voted for members of the House of Representatives voted Republican—50 or almost 51 percent. It is because of districting, gerrymandering—and I do not mean to use this in a pejorative way—that the House has a Democratic majority.

MR. CUTLER: Take a broader sweep of history. We do this again and again. For half the time of the last seven, now eight, administrations, we have put the Congress in the hands of a different party than the presidency.

One suggestion that has been made, one that could be accomplished without a constitutional amendment, is that, either by the will of one or both parties or by a congressional preemptive statute, there should be a single primary or state convention time for the nomination of candidates to the House and Senate. Once nominated, those candidates, together with the holdover senators of the same party, would meet in a convention to nominate candidates for president and vice president, who might very well come from among their number.

That suggestion is very close, as I understand it, to the original development of the parties when the Democratic–Republican, Federalist, or Whig, members of the sitting House and Senate met together to choose the candidates for president and vice president of the party.

MR. DALY: I believe we have broadly presented the subject and also the issues concerned, and that it is now time to go to the question and answer session. May I have the first question, please?

MEL ELFIN, *Newsweek* magazine: Mr. Cutler suggested that if the president and the Congress reach a stalemate, under his system, they would necessarily have to resign and have new elections. How would that contribute to the efficiency of government and speed in dealing with foreign policy issues? Would it not put us under a kind of Fourth Republic?

MR. CUTLER: I did not suggest any of the proposals that are listed. I simply tried to catalog them. The present French constitution, as you may know, empowers the president to call for new elections in the Parliament, not the other way around.

One possibility that has been suggested is a two-way street. The president could exercise a constitutional power to dissolve the Congress and call for new elections; a majority, or perhaps two-thirds, of the Congress, only in that event, could call for a new presidential election at the same time.

That power is a sort of political nuclear weapon, but its existence might break many stalemates because of the distaste of the members of Congress for having new elections. That is the theory of it. Of course, it could only work if we had an electoral system—and we would have to adopt it as part of any such change—that could produce a new government, as in Britain or in the constitutional parliamentary systems, within thirty to sixty days. The incumbent government would stay in until the election is held.

DR. WILSON: Once you start unraveling this sweater, it all starts coming apart. You cannot change one part of the system without, as Mr. Cutler has indicated, thinking about changing all parts of the system. If we have the president calling a congressional election or the Congress forcing a presidential election, we have to change the party system. This means we have to change the degree of control the national government has over state governments, because ultimately they control the local party systems. We have to force a different kind of primary or convention system. This alters the relationship between the state governments and the parties. I cannot, because I lack the wit, imagine all of the additional permutations that are implied. My point is simple: There are no simple changes in the Constitution.

MR. ELFIN: Also, Mr. Cutler, does it not work only in a system where the party is unified over principle, where there are smaller constituencies, and in more unified, homogeneous countries? In our country of 220 million people and so many diverse political interests, our political parties really could not sit down and subscribe to a single body of values. Look at the fighting that goes on over a political platform in a convention, which is the party's least common denominator. It would be hard to find a group of congressmen and a president of either political party who could sit down and agree on a balanced program. It would be exceedingly hard and would lead to incredible instability.

Concerning what Mr. Wilson said, if we look at the separation of powers, does it not also apply to fifty state governments in our country, which also have a comparable kind of system and not a parliamentary system? Would you suggest that they move to a parliamentary system?

MR. CUTLER: To take your last question first, other federal systems—the German system and the Canadian system—have parliamentary governments at the top. Of course, they have repetitions of it at each level. Those governments work quite well.

It is quite true that the federal system is an added complication for us, one in which the virtues may still outweigh the costs. For any of these various measures, however, the whole point is to induce the kind of shared political fate between the majority of legislators, as a group, and the president that would lead them to agree on a balanced program. If we are to accept the proposition that we are so diverse we cannot agree on a balanced program and, therefore, we cannot have one, I really fear for what will happen to this country. If we cannot have a balanced program, we cannot control our budget.

My main thesis, though, is not to advance any one of these solutions. I agree that each one of them has a lot of problems to it. My main thesis is to try to establish the proposition that we need to do better in forming a government, that we do not do it well today, that structural problems stand in the way—particularly the lack of a shared political fate between the legislators and the president or the candidate for president—and that this is what we need to focus on.

MR. SILBERMAN: I do not think we could define a balanced program. That is a very illusory word. It suggests some kind of objective standard and there is none. Mr. Cutler's balanced program would be anathema to me.

To go back to Mr. Brandon's point, we cannot trust anybody, even the president, to define the national interest—except me, and I do not think you would give me that constitutional power. [Laughter.]

MR. CUTLER: It is not a question of whether Program A is better than Program B, whether more defense and less social welfare is better than less defense and more social welfare, or whether we ought to lower taxes to increase productivity or have the federal government do something. It is that *somebody's* program is given a chance. What we have today is *nobody's* program. No one is prepared to endorse what we have today. I will wager you anything that President Reagan will not be able to carry out his program, however he chooses to

19

define it. He will say, "You can't blame me," and the Congress will do the same thing.

MR. BRANDON: I only want to add that Mr. Elfin defined the reasons why the British parliamentary system could not be applied in this country.

MR. DALY: The diversity of our society?

MR. BRANDON: Yes.

WALTER BERNS, American Enterprise Institute: Mr. Cutler, I have a question for you, too. It seems to me that you exaggerate the difficulties the president faces, both in foreign policy and in domestic policy. By that, of course, I mean your suggestion that he faces difficulties that are part of the system of separated powers and that these difficulties really prevent him from doing what has to be done at any particular time.

But take two questions, one of foreign policy, one of domestic policy, arising during the last administration when you were there. Could it fairly be said that it was the separation of powers that prevented President Carter from responding properly at the time the hostages were seized? And, in the field of domestic policy, when you complain about the inability to get a decisive national-interest budget, can it fairly be said that it was the separation of powers that prevented President Carter from getting a budget adopted? If the answer to that is yes, which budget do you have in mind?

MR. CUTLER: In the case of the hostage crisis, which united this country and in which Congress probably would have done anything the president asked, the separation of powers was not a factor. I disagree with your conclusions that the president adopted the wrong policies. I have not heard any other policies put forward, either before or after the fact, that had much of a chance of achieving any different result from what we now have.

I will give you some other examples. I will give you the invasion of Afghanistan and the need, or at least the need perceived by the president, to provide some additional aid to Pakistan. We ran into the problems of legislative requirements that neither military nor various types of economic aid could be given to Pakistan unless Pakistan had given certain nonproliferation assurances, which could not be obtained. In the case of draft registration, the president, the head of our government in foreign policy, determined that one appropriate signal to the Soviets was that at the very least, we were going to prepare for the possible need for a draft. The difficulty of obtaining draft registration approval, even for a $20 million appropriation—that is all that was at stake—took so long as to blunt the message we were trying to send and proved almost insurmountable.

So far as the budgets are concerned, to take a favorite Reagan subject, defense budgets, it is a fact that for the past ten years, Congress has legislated a lower defense budget than the president asked for. It is a fact that for the last ten years no president has gotten either the net budget results or the mix within a budget that he wanted, nor has any legislator or legislative leader of either party gotten the composite mix that he wanted. No one can be held accountable for our failure, the collective failure, to prevent these enormous budget deficits over the years.

DR. BERNS: May I respond to that? Your first response is interesting. That is to say, your response to my first point about the seizure of the hostages. You said that on that particular occasion it was certainly not the separation of powers that prevented the president from doing what might be done, because there was such a unanimity of view in the country, and that any policy that made sense probably would have been supported.

MR. CUTLER: Even some that did not make sense.

DR. BERNS: Yes, probably some that would not have made sense. That is exactly the sort of thing that Mr. Wilson was talking about earlier. When, indeed, that kind of unanimity behind a particular policy is understood to be or is present and when the country agrees that a particular problem has to be dealt with, the separation of powers is not an insuperable barrier to the achievement of policy.

MR. CUTLER: That is entirely right.

DR. BERNS: Therefore, I conclude by repeating what I said at the beginning. You exaggerate the difficulties posed by the separation of powers.

MR. CUTLER: I tried not to. I tried to point out in my article that when the system has worked, when we have been able to legislate and execute a policy for dealing with a situation—such as the Great Depression and World War II under FDR, the early days of the Johnson Great Society, and perhaps the early days of Wilson's own

New Freedom—that when there is a great consensus in the country, usually brought on by a great crisis, an external shock, the assassination of a beloved president, whatever it might be, for a while the system works.

But those are very rare times in this century. When we think of when the system worked, when we think of great presidents who accomplished something in their administration, we tend to think of Wilson, FDR, perhaps Lyndon Johnson, and perhaps Eisenhower, although he governed successfully for eight years by running the most limited possible government. Remove Eisenhower from the list, because his theory was to do as little as possible; although that worked in 1952, it would not work in the world we live in today. The economy now is an integral part of a worldwide system, to most of which the writ of our Constitution and our government just does not reach at all. It is not possible any longer to let our little free enterprise system, unmanaged, flower in a world of managed and competing world economies.

It does seem to me that the fact that the system has worked when there were great crises and great consensus tends to prove my point. Most of the time, we do not have 80–20 or 70–30 majorities; we have a series of issues on which the public splits 55–45—the environment, whether to restrict auto imports—and we have to be able to govern in those situations, as well.

MR. SILBERMAN: I would like to respond to Mr. Cutler's last remark. His comment about the Eisenhower administration reflects what is the underlying reality of his thesis. It is posed in terms of a procedural reform, but in fact it is based on certain subjective notions of what proper policy is. In his article, it is quite clear. He explains all the things the Carter administration could not get done, which he thinks should have been done, and then he describes them as balanced. Then he says because we could not do that, there is a fundamental defect in American government, and it has to be our Constitution. It is very difficult, reading his article or hearing him now, to think of any neutral question that somehow can be described outside of a subjective policy view.

Earlier, when I said one man's balanced program is another man's extreme program, he made his second point, which is that there ought to be political accountability and everybody ought to have to stand together under a single program—the Congress, the Senate, the president. As a matter of fact, we had an election in the latter part of 1980, in which that turned out to be more true than many thought was likely or possible. A number of senators were turned out of office, as well as the president, for voting for and adopting certain policies that the majority of the American people thought were wrong.

MR. CUTLER: We shall see whether the majority of the American people or the majority of Congress thinks the policies are wrong. Governor Reagan should have the opportunity to carry out his program, or at least the Republican party should have the opportunity to carry out its program.

MR. SILBERMAN: Will you guarantee your support?

MR. CUTLER: I will guarantee to try to give you the chance. It cannot be a do-nothing program. Programs are now in place. There are ongoing, continuing drains on the budget in place, which you must dismantle to carry out your program, and you will not be able to do it because of a structural fault and the fact that legislators are not sharing President Reagan's political fate. Both he and they will be able to say in the end, "Although we didn't get anything done and inflation is still at the same level, it's not our fault."

RUTH HINERFELD, League of Women Voters: I would like to pursue this question of a national consensus. As Dr. Wilson said, the public interest is not necessarily the sum of private interests, and, as Mr. Cutler has pointed out, national consensus only seems to emerge in times of great national adversity. What institutional improvements or changes can there be, short of the kinds of changes Mr. Cutler advocates, that would help the nation in its search for consensus? I say "search for consensus," recognizing that consensus, by itself, may not necessarily be of the highest value. In the absence of the search for consensus, however, we seem to be afflicted with many of the problems that have been characterized as difficulties of the present time—fragmentation, extreme self-interest, single interest groups. These things, of course, have been blamed on such developments as the weakening of the parties as institutions for mediation, changes in legislative and executive relations, changes in the leadership, and so-called reforms in both houses of the Congress.

Are there any alternatives in institution-building that will help us in that search for a national consensus?

DR. WILSON: I am not confident there are institutional strategies to achieve that objective. Among the reasons why there is not only disagreement but in some quarters disaffection about the government

23

is that the government has promised more than it could achieve and has done so at the expense of inflating the currency and harming, in a very visible way, a style of life that most Americans thought was their birthright.

The source of my ultimate skepticism about Mr. Cutler's proposal is doubt that institutional reforms of the sort he proposes would do anything more than feed this process by enlarging expectations, enlarging the role of the president as a national leader conducting not an election but a plebiscite. The president's proposals would be put forward, based on assembling a coalition by offering as much as possible to as many as possible. Though this would sound good in the short run, it would lead to enlarged, and ultimately frustrated, expectations.

The problem is that government is too large. Although you and I might not agree—I am not certain about that—I am looking for ways of making government more modest and, at the same time, more moderate. Perhaps this can be done by constitutional limitations on spending; perhaps it can be done by other, less drastic means to force choices. I am not convinced, however, that this process will be facilitated by enhancing the power of the executive to ask for a yes-or-no vote on his program, because those programs that have received yes votes have produced this problem we now face.

MR. CUTLER: I agree with Dr. Wilson as to what is wise policy for the federal government. I also would like to see policy that is more modest and much more forthright in recognizing that we cannot have energy self-sufficiency and a perfect environment and a productive industry at the same time.

My difficulty with what he suggests is that it will be very difficult for a president elected on a mandate of having more moderate government to carry out that policy. It will be very hard, given our present system, to defeat the particular single interest groups that Ms. Hinerfeld referred to. It will be very hard to put into effect any program that any one of us is prepared to endorse.

In the end, the public will look for the party that will say, "We do intend to discipline ourselves. If you elect us to office, both the presidency and the legislature, we will stick together and carry out this program. If the majority whip goes against the leadership and the president on a particular matter, he will lose his office of whip," something we do not do today in our system.

HERBERT STEIN, American Enterprise Institute: I would like to ask three short questions.

Mr. Cutler seems to regard as an essential criterion for a good policy that one person, the president or even a congressman, regard it as the best of all possible policies. An alternative position is that a policy that very many people think is the second best or the third best might be better than a policy that some one person thinks is the first best. I wonder why he thinks that the criterion should be that one person think the policy is the first best.

MR. CUTLER: I did not mean one person, I meant the group that we elect to govern; and I do not mean one policy in the sense of one energy policy being better than another policy. I am talking about the balance to be achieved in going about the pursuit of our very many conflicting and competing goals, every one of which has a great deal to be said in its favor. I come back, in particular, to this issue of the budget.

DR. STEIN: I would like to ask a question about the budget. Most people would agree that our governing processes have many deficiencies and that many of them focus on the budget. I would like to hear some comment on the possibilities for reform, other than such radical, structural ones as have been discussed here.

After all, we did make a very big change in 1974 in the budgetary process, with which there has been rather limited experience, and I would be interested in any comments on whether that has improved the outcome at all. I would suggest that the outcome is not noticeably better in other countries with structurally different systems. In any case, the budgetary process still has a lot of room for change. We made a rather unwise decision in 1974 to take away the president's power to withhold or impound funds, which would have been a way to limit things. We could do something about the item veto, about long-range budgeting—things that seem simpler to me than a constitutional convention.

MR. CUTLER: Again, I am not proposing a constitutional convention. Most of the budget reforms you mention probably would require constitutional reform—unless Congress adopted the habit of putting in every piece of legislation, every piece of appropriation legislation, for example, permission for an item veto.

One could think of a provision, which I understand is in the German constitution, that the legislature may not enact a budget or a set of appropriations greater than proposed by the cabinet, by the government. I believe the Canadians have some similar provision in their constitution. How we would arrive at that, short of constitutional reform, is very difficult to imagine. A really determined Congress, a party that imposes discipline on its members, a return perhaps to the tools of power that Lyndon Johnson and Sam Rayburn possessed, would get us a long way in that direction, but it is very hard to turn history back on reforms of that type. The congressional budget process is almost in disintegration today, as you know.

DR. STEIN: Many people thought it would not survive this long; I would not be so desperate about it. A question I did not hear discussed has to do with this change in the kind of thing that the government does, which has affected the balance of power between the executive and the legislative branches in a very fundamental way. That is the enormous explosion of government regulation, which the Congress has no possible way of exercising any control over and which has inevitably made an enormous shift of power toward the executive. I wonder whether anybody has any suggestions for ways of redressing that imbalance.

MR. CUTLER: I am going to move right over with you and Mr. Silberman on that proposition. I have proposed, myself, that the president should assert power over the executive branch regulatory agencies, and even—if the Congress gives him power—over the independent agencies. Once more, however, to be able to do any of these things, you need discipline between an executive, even one so disposed, and the majority in the Congress to accomplish it. Every regulatory agency, with its single mission, has behind it a single-mission congressional committee and single-mission constituencies. It is very hard, even for a determined president, to impose on that agency the need for balance in considering other national goals.

DR. WILSON: I am ordinarily not cast in the role of reformer, but if reforms are to be sought, we should seek them from within the American experience on the basis of those institutional arrangements to which the American people have become accustomed. We should not reach overseas for an approximation of the parliamentary system; we should look at state and city governments in this country and ask what modifications in federal arrangements already tested at the city and state levels might commend themselves. Many governors have, in fact, line-item vetos awarded to them by state constitutions. Many city charters deny to city councils the right to increase the executive budget.

None of them, so far as I know, allows the governor or the mayor to force a new election, or vice versa, nor does any require the abolition of the separation of powers. These modest changes, which would require, as Mr. Cutler says, constitutional change, are the sorts of changes on which we could focus attention with a greater confidence that we know what we would get as a result.

MR. SILBERMAN: That is an excellent point.

At one point in Mr. Cutler's article he advocates that the president have control of executive branch agencies, and he has previously described that in a more elaborate way. Although we have certainly indicated a disagreement between Mr. Cutler and me, I thoroughly agree with the notion that having independent regulatory agencies is a constitutional anomaly, because in many respects it is in defiance of democratic theory. These independent agencies are not responsive to any democratic process—not to the Congress, not to the president. I would go further on that and suggest, as I did earlier—and here Mr. Cutler probably would not agree with me—that many of our problems, including many of the frustrations of the executive, come about because of avowed and open judicial policy making, which was not contemplated by the Founders of the Constitution.

MR. CUTLER: Let me cite Paul MacAvoy as an example for the proposition that more new regulatory agencies, and some of those with the greatest impact from the cost-imposing standpoint, were created during the Republican Nixon and Ford administrations than during the Kennedy, Johnson, and Carter administrations combined. I hasten to say, as you would say, that most of that was done because there were Democratic Congresses during those administrations, but that proves my point. We had not formed a government capable of carrying out a policy during those administrations. That is when the Environmental Protection Agency was originated by a Nixon executive order; that is when the Occupational Safety and Health Administration was originated; that is when the Consumer Product Safety Commission was originated. They are all children of this bastard form of government we have, in which the president might go one way and the legislature, or parts of it, are free to go another.

JOHN FORSTER, Initiative America: My question is directed toward Mr. Silberman.

Most Americans would agree with you that our system of checks and balances and separation of powers is one of our strongest assets. If we can assume, though, that the problems in government today occur when our branches of government fail to come to a consensus or when they adopt a policy that the vast majority of Americans disagrees with, would you support extending our system of checks and balances and separation of powers to allowing voters to propose legislative solutions themselves to keep our branches of government in balance when they are in paralysis or in disagreement with Americans?

MR. SILBERMAN: I had always been somewhat hostile to initiative legislation until Proposition 13 was passed in California. [Laughter.]

Then, I was tempted to change my procedural views in accordance with the subjective results, as I have accused Mr. Cutler of doing. I restrained myself, however, and I am still opposed to the notion of initiative, certainly at the national level. I like the republican form of government.

DR. WILSON: I agree with Mr. Silberman.

MR. CUTLER: I do not have many such opportunities, so I want to concur in Mr. Silberman's idea. The principal problem with initiative legislation is that we lose the benefits of the legislative process—the possibilities for debate, constructive amendment, and compromise. We are stuck with the initial wording of the initiative, bad as it may be.

MR. DALY: Would you like to concur in this also, Mr. Brandon?

MR. BRANDON: Yes. A referendum bypasses the democratic process.

MR. DALY: This concludes another public policy forum, presented by the American Enterprise Institute for Public Policy Research. On behalf of AEI, our hearty thanks to the distinguished and expert panelists, Mr. Henry O. Brandon, Mr. Lloyd N. Cutler, Mr. Laurence H. Silberman, and Dr. James Q. Wilson. Our thanks, too, to the guests in our audience for their participation.

Suggestions for Further Reading

Brandon, Henry. "The U.S. Constitution: Is It Time for Reform?" *Washington Star*, September 18, 1980.

Cutler, Lloyd N. "To Form a Government." *Foreign Affairs*, Fall 1980.

Diamond, Martin; Fisk, Winston Mills; and Garfinkel, Herbert. *The Democratic Republic*. 2nd ed. Chicago: Rand McNally and Co., 1971, pp. 103–111, 159–163.

Greider, William. "Our Elites' Malaise: All This Democracy." *Washington Post*, November 12, 1980.

Kilpatrick, James J. "The Way We Govern: Some Radical Proposals." *Washington Star*, November 19, 1980.

Mann, Thomas E., and Ornstein, Norman J. "Congress and the President." *Foreign Affairs*, Winter 1980/81.

Wilson, James, Q. "American Politics, Then and Now." *Commentary*, February 1979.

2

War Powers and the Constitution

Dick Cheney
John Charles Daly
Lee H. Hamilton
Charles McC. Mathias, Jr.
Brent Scowcroft

with an appendix by Gerald R. Ford

J OHN CHARLES DALY, former ABC News chief: This public policy forum, part of a series presented by the American Enterprise Institute, is concerned with the division of war powers between the
Congress and the president. Our Founding Fathers, after much debate, preferred not to spell out that division precisely in the Constitution, but in the last three decades Congress has been determined to
interpret and define it. Our subject: War Powers and the Constitution.

Many resolutions and bills have been exhaustively debated in Congress, and it is not extreme to say that the mountain has long labored
and brought forth no consensus on precisely where war powers lie.
The passage over President Nixon's veto of the War Powers Resolution of 1973 served principally to establish a new point of departure for
the continuing debate. That debate has been supported on both sides
by a phalanx of historians, members of Congress, academicians, current and former cabinet and subcabinet officers, and others.

In broad strokes the Constitution stipulates that the Congress shall
have the power to declare war, to raise and support armies, and to
provide and maintain a navy; the president shall be the commander in
chief of the armed forces. The Constitutional Convention of 1787,
hammering out the language on war powers, discussed granting Congress the power to "make war," but ultimately it decided on the power
to "declare war," seemingly on the grounds that the conduct of war is
an executive, not a congressional, function. Again in broad strokes,
the War Powers Resolution of 1973 requires the president (1) to consult
with the Congress "in every possible instance" before U.S. armed
forces enter hostilities or situations of imminent hostilities; (2) to re-
port to the Congress within forty-eight hours when forces are so
committed; and (3) to terminate the engagement within sixty days if
Congress has not declared war or specifically authorized continued
use of the armed forces. Finally, it allows Congress within those sixty
days to direct the president to withdraw U.S. forces by a concurrent
resolution passed by both houses, but not requiring the president's
signature.

It should be noted that in the nineteenth century it became accepted practice, with relatively little objection, for the president to use American forces in limited actions, mainly in our own hemisphere. In the twentieth century, with its two world wars, with the peculiar new animal the undeclared war, with the Soviet commitment to global communism producing cataclysm on every continent, with the memories we all have of Korea, Vietnam, the Cuban missile crisis, and the Berlin airlift, with the troubles in Latin America and the Middle East, where in truth lie the security and best interests of the United States in the allocation of war powers?

To chart a course out of this difficulty, we have a distinguished panel: Representative Lee H. Hamilton, Democrat of Indiana, has been a member of Congress since 1965. He is a member of the House Foreign Affairs Committee and serves on the Permanent Select Committee on Intelligence. Senator Charles McC. Mathias, Jr., Republican and senior senator from Maryland, is a member of the Senate Foreign Relations Committee and is second ranking member of the Judiciary Committee. Representative Dick Cheney, Republican of Wyoming, served in the Ford administration as White House chief of staff. Elected to the Congress in 1978, Representative Cheney was chosen by his colleagues to serve as chairman of the House Republican Policy Committee. He is also a member of the House Committee on Interior and Insular Affairs. Lieutenant General Brent Scowcroft, before retiring from military service in the air force, served in the White House as President Ford's national security adviser. More recently General Scowcroft served as chairman of President Reagan's Commission on Strategic Forces. In 1981 he was codirector of AEI's project on American Vital Interests in Regions of Conflict.

Let us hear first the views of our thirty-eighth president on the War Powers Resolution and the problems of trying to sort out the prerogatives and responsibilities of the Congress and the executive. Remember, the act was passed over President Nixon's veto in 1973. Gerald Ford succeeded to the presidency in 1974 and almost immediately had to confront the issue of war powers. (See the remarks of President Gerald Ford in the appendix.)

I would pose the same question to each of the panelists: Has the world changed so radically in two hundred years that the Congress should attempt what our Founding Fathers were not willing to do in writing the Constitution, specifically to define and catalog the prerogatives and powers of the Congress and the executive in the exercise of war powers?

CHARLES McC. MATHIAS, JR., U.S. senator (Republican, Maryland): I would take issue with the question as it is framed, because it seems to

34

me that the Congress is not doing anything novel at the end of two centuries, anything different from what the Founding Fathers contemplated. The authors of the Constitution made it very clear where the power over war and peace would rest. It is true that they made the president commander in chief of the armed forces, but they vested the decision on war and peace solely in the Congress of the United States. They gave the Congress the power to make rules and regulations for the governance of the armed forces, to make rules for captures on land or water, to issue letters of marque, authorizing a warlike act by private vessels. So the Constitution vests a panoply of power in the Congress that makes it clear that the founders wanted the Congress to control issues of war and peace. What the War Powers Resolution does is merely to implement in a modern framework what I believe to be a very clear constitutional purpose.

DICK CHENEY, U.S. representative (Republican, Wyoming): I take strong exception to the view of my friend and colleague Senator Mathias. I believe that the declaration of war is almost an outmoded concept under virtually any set of circumstances we can conceive of under which a president would decide to commit troops to combat. In many respects the War Powers Resolution is a legacy of the Vietnam War, very much like the Trade and Neutrality Act of the late 1930s. It is a statute adopted in an effort to keep us out of the next war based on a misperception of how we got into the last one. It was put on the books with the expectation that if it had been on the books in 1964 and 1965, this nation would never have been involved in Southeast Asia. I believe that that is not the case. Congress consistently and continually supported our involvement in Southeast Asia, and the War Powers Resolution has not changed that. I believe very firmly that the War Powers Resolution is an unwise and virtually unworkable intrusion by the legislative branch into the powers and prerogatives the president needs to lead the United States in a very dangerous and hostile world.

LEE H. HAMILTON, U.S. representative (Democrat, Indiana): I support the War Powers Resolution. Edward Corwin, the great constitutional scholar, said that the Constitution is an invitation to the Congress and the president to struggle for the privilege of conducting American foreign policy. The War Powers Resolution simply reflects that struggle. Its purpose is to guarantee that the Congress and the president will exercise their collective judgment on the most important question faced by government, and that is whether or not the country goes to war. The extreme complexity of the modern world, the very rapid growth of America's responsibilities in that world, and the ambiguity of many international conflicts demand that the Congress and the president exercise their collective judgment on the critical question of whether or not to go to war. To put the matter succinctly, in this kind of a world Lebanon is not Pearl Harbor, and when a decision calls for the best that we can summon, it ought not to be made by one man or woman, even if that man or woman is the president of the United States. It ought to be a collective judgment.

BRENT SCOWCROFT, lieutenant general–retired (U.S. Air Force): It is not so much that the world has changed in two hundred years as that the United States and its role in the world have changed substantially. The Constitution did not legislate a government designed for maximum efficiency. It legislated a government designed to protect the rights of the individual against an overweening government, and it does that very well. The problem is that the inefficiency that kind of freedom-protecting innovation dictates makes it very difficult for a world power to discharge its responsibilities.

As Representative Hamilton stated, in the struggle between the executive and the legislature for predominance, the balance has shifted throughout our history from one to the other. The War Powers Resolution reflects a time when, after a series of dynamic and activist presidents, the presidency was beset both by our involvement in Vietnam and by Watergate. The Congress in effect seized an opportunity to change the balance that had prevailed essentially since the administration of Franklin Roosevelt. We must find ways for the executive and the legislature to cooperate in the discharge of the awesome business of conflict, but I think the War Powers Resolution, in the way it attempts to achieve that, ties the hands of the president and makes conflict more likely.

SENATOR MATHIAS: I agree with Representative Cheney that the War Powers Resolution grew out of the experience of Vietnam. I lived through that as a member of Congress. I voted for the Gulf of Tonkin resolution, and I think it is fair to say that most of us who did vote for it felt, as the facts were revealed, that we had been bamboozled and that there was no mechanism by which the Congress could come to grips with the situation once the resolution had been passed. Once when I was riding in an automobile with President Johnson and expressed some doubts about the war, he said, "You voted for this resolution: now, if you've got the guts, step up and introduce a resolution to repeal it." And he reached in his pocket and pulled out a copy. We were really without a way to debate the issues; once troops are committed and casualties are being sustained and the patriotism of the country is aroused, it is very hard to get hold of.

The War Powers Resolution provides a mechanism and a process by which the Congress can periodically review our involvement in foreign military ventures. I think this is entirely consistent with what the writers of the Constitution proposed. James Madison, who probably knew more about the Constitution than any other man who ever lived, once wrote to Thomas Jefferson that the Constitution assumes what the history of all governments demonstrates: that the executive is the branch of power most interested in war and most prone to it. It has accordingly, with studied care, vested the question of war in the legislature.

REPRESENTATIVE CHENEY: I have to take exception to Senator Mathias. I think the War Powers Resolution—

SENATOR MATHIAS: You can take exception to me, but you would have trouble taking exception to Madison.

REPRESENTATIVE CHENEY: Obviously there are differences in our interpretations of what the Constitution provides with respect to whether the president or the legislature has prime authority in war powers. I think most members of Congress, even those like me who have serious problems with the War Powers Resolution, believe that the language of the resolution, which speaks of consultation and notification, is perfectly appropriate. It is the notion that Congress can terminate a commitment of forces after a very short period that bothers me a great deal.

I look on the Congress as all too often swayed by the public opinion of the moment. There is no procedure that would enable Congress to be an equal partner with the president, in light of all the resources available to him, in making broad policy decisions that must hold for a year or two. We have seen, for example, the Speaker of the House at the outset call the Grenada mission "gunboat diplomacy"; within two weeks he had changed his mind and concluded that President Reagan had done exactly the right thing in sending troops into Grenada.

SENATOR MATHIAS: He was right the first time.

REPRESENTATIVE CHENEY: Unfortunately Congress is a pretty weak reed to lean on for that kind of decision making. I would also argue that if the War Powers Resolution had been on the books in 1964 when the Gulf of Tonkin resolution was adopted, it would not have altered the outcome at all. Congress did indeed have the opportunity throughout our involvement in Southeast Asia to reject the course we were engaged on, but year after year it appropriated the funds for that exercise. I think it is a misreading of history to suggest that the War

Powers Resolution might have altered the outcome in Southeast Asia.

REPRESENTATIVE HAMILTON: I think the real question is whether a decision about war making ought to be made by one person or by the president and the Congress together. That seems to me to be at the heart of it, and the War Powers Resolution simply says that the Congress is going to participate in such a decision. Why shouldn't it? The guiding principle is that a democracy should go to war only with the consent of the people, as expressed by their elected representatives. So I think the War Powers Resolution is wholly consistent with the Constitution and with the intentions of the Founding Fathers. General Scowcroft spoke about tying the hands of the president. Quite frankly, that is one of the things we want to do. We want to make the president stop, think, and listen before he commits us to war.

REPRESENTATIVE CHENEY: The most important decision that anyone is going to make about the use of our military forces would obviously be a decision to use nuclear weapons. At that point Congress, even under the War Powers Resolution, is irrelevant. We have made a decision to build those weapons and to give the president as commander in chief control of them; if he decided tomorrow, because of an impending Soviet attack, to launch those weapons, Congress would have no role whatsoever. I think the idea of Congress sharing in the decision to declare war under such circumstances is almost meaningless.

REPRESENTATIVE HAMILTON: There may always be an emergency. The president may be faced with a decision when he has been told by his staff that the missiles are coming and he has only ten or fifteen or twenty minutes to respond. Clearly that would be an emergency. I do not think anyone would deny that the president ought to act then without trying to find the Speaker of the House or the majority leader of the Senate. But in an ordinary situation he ought to consult with the Congress before he goes to war. I believe that the War Powers Resolution is beneficial because it brings Congress into the decision on war, something it does not like to face.

REPRESENTATIVE CHENEY: Is there a recent example of a president's failing to consult before committing troops?

REPRESENTATIVE HAMILTON: Look what happened with Grenada. The president called in the Speaker and the majority leader at 8:00 P.M. He did not consult with them. The Speaker has said they were informed that the marines were landing at 5:30 the next morning. There was no consultation; it was just a matter of informing, and informing is not consultation. At 8:00 P.M. the Speaker learned about it, the rest of us learned about it from the newspaper, and the marines went in at 5:30. That is not consultation. When President Carter sent the troops to Iran for a rescue mission, he did not consult with the Congress. He just went ahead and did it.

REPRESENTATIVE CHENEY: It might have cost hundreds of lives if we had had the usual dialogue and debate about whether Congress would authorize action.

GENERAL SCOWCROFT: If we could broaden the discussion beyond the Congress, there are a number of other elements to consider. I want to underscore what Representative Cheney says: the Congress already has adequate resources to restrain the president. It does control the purse strings; it does raise and maintain armies. If it does not like what the executive is doing, it has all the power it needs to stop the president's actions.

REPRESENTATIVE HAMILTON: That is a very slow power; it takes Congress a long time to do that. The advantage of the War Powers Resolution is that, within the sixty-day period or the extended ninety-day period, the Congress has to act to approve or disapprove.

GENERAL SCOWCROFT: No, it does not have to act. That is one of the key points. If it does not act, it makes a decision by its inaction. That seems to me a supine way for the Congress to work its will. In the real world the president sometimes has to introduce forces into an area to try to prevent a conflict, to stabilize a region, or to prevent something from happening by demonstrating our resolve. Telling our potential opponents that all they have to do is wait sixty days and see what happens undercuts his ability to demonstrate the kind of resolve that could prevent a conflict.

REPRESENTATIVE HAMILTON: I disagree with that, General, because the act strengthens the decision to commit troops. If the president commits troops and does not have the support of the Congress or of the American people, he will not be able to sustain that commitment, and he will not be able to keep those troops there. We have learned that lesson very, very hard. How does he get the support of the American people? One of the ways is to have the support of the Congress.

MR. DALY: Let me ask you to focus on Lebanon. Senator Mathias, you played a major part in a compromise that was worked out, the terms of which were never specific, on whether the War Powers Resolution should apply to the president's commitment of marines to the peace-keeping force in Lebanon. That is a peculiar framework to consider because the president did not introduce troops into Lebanon to engage in hostilities but to join in a peace-keeping force with other nations. How do we address that situation?

SENATOR MATHIAS: Let me first add a footnote to Representative Cheney's comment that consulting Congress would bring about thousands of deaths because Congress cannot keep a secret. I very much disagree. In the Grenada situation the lack of consultation was compounded by the president's decision to advise the prime minister of Great Britain before he advised the Speaker of the House of Representatives and the majority leader of the Senate. That really causes me some trouble.

But to get down to Lebanon. I think the War Powers Resolution made a very positive contribution—though far from perfect—to the management of the Lebanese situation. There were some ambiguities both in the way the situation came about and in the structure of our response. But we made it very clear in the compromise that the troops on the beach were to be limited to the number who were there on the day the resolution passed. There were ambiguities about offshore naval forces, but there was absolutely no question about the troops on the beach; it was totally specific. We are protected from the kind of insidious growth that occurred in Vietnam, where we went from a few hundred advisers to 500,000 troops with only a kind of indirect congressional authorization: Congress provided their pay and their rations and thereby indirectly authorized their presence. But if we go beyond the number of Marines who were originally in Lebanon, there has to be real congressional consultation, more than just advice.

REPRESENTATIVE HAMILTON: Mr. Daly, did you say that the War Powers Resolution was not implemented in the Lebanon situation?

MR. DALY: No, I said that there seems to be some confusion about whether or not it was applied or is accepted as applied by both Congress and the president.

REPRESENTATIVE HAMILTON: It is very clear in the resolution that was passed that section 4A1 of the War Powers Resolution was implemented. President Reagan, when he signed it, did show some reservations; he obviously had some question about it, but he did sign it. This was the first full use of the War Powers Resolution as I understand it.

GENERAL SCOWCROFT: It seems to me that, with respect to Lebanon, the question is not that clear. Legislation has been passed and agreed to and so on, but section 4A expressly talks about forces introduced. Those forces originally went in without any idea that hostilities were imminent. That hostilities or the possibility of hostilities subsequently developed seems to me to point to a very different kind of legal question.

REPRESENTATIVE HAMILTON: The War Powers Resolution permits the president or the Congress to trigger the section of the act concerning the sixty-day limit. In this case the Congress triggered it, started the time clock ticking, and the president accepted that. That stands as a historical precedent of major importance—for a president to accept the War Powers Resolution.

GENERAL SCOWCROFT: He did not accept the War Powers Resolution.

REPRESENTATIVE HAMILTON: The president accepted it by signing the Lebanon resolution. He made a statement about his reservations, but he signed the resolution, and it is the law of the land. The law specifically triggers the War Powers Resolution.

GENERAL SCOWCROFT: Representative Hamilton, many presidents have signed many bills while stating that there are constitutional problems. That does not mean that the president acquiesces.

REPRESENTATIVE CHENEY: That two such obviously intelligent and distinguished gentlemen as General Scowcroft and Representative Hamilton cannot even agree on what we did in the Lebanon resolution strikes me as pretty hard evidence that the War Powers Resolution is a very difficult piece of legislation and probably unworkable. I would certainly support General Scowcroft's views on what the administration did. I was fascinated by the debate on the issue when it came to the floor of the House because the debate had nothing to do with whether we should be there. Nobody offered an alternative that said everybody out now. The alternatives were 60-day, 90-day, 180-day, or eighteen-month limits, and often the debate over how long it should be had very little to do with the substance of the policy and much more to do with the posturing of my colleagues and whether anyone could build a majority for six months instead of nine months. It is a bad way to make policy. I also think the limit on numbers of troops on the beach is very unwise. If we are going to commit military force in a potentially hostile situation, one of the keys to its having any effect is the uncertainty created in the minds of our adversaries. If we say at the outset that we are going to commit troops but can have no more than 1,600 on the beach under any foreseeable circumstances, it defeats the purpose of having troops there in the first place.

SENATOR MATHIAS: Two points. One is the time factor. Of course, we are not talking about an absolute termination of the operation but about a period of time after which the Congress will make a review and there will be further consultation and, as Lee Hamilton says, a joint decision by the Congress and the executive whether the operation should be continued. That is a point that never came in Vietnam in a formal, structured way, and that is what was missing in the Vietnam debate. The executive could simply roll over the Congress. In fact, my good friend and colleague Mel Laird, who was secretary of defense, once said he did not even need appropriations, he could use the Food and Forage Act and just keep going without appropriations. That kind of experience makes some periodic congressional review desirable. I thought that six months was about the right time limit.

The other point I want to make is this. As Representative Cheney says, if we say we are going to get out in a limited time, that may make the adversary procrastinate and not come to terms with reality. In the Lebanese situation, however, not having a limit could make our friends there rest on their arms and not really engage in the hard political process necessary to bring about a reconciliation of the conflict. The longer they keep us there, the longer they do not have to come to terms with the reality of political life there. So there are two sides to the question of the uncertainties created by having or not having a time limit.

MR. DALY: What about the big constitutional question—the provision in the War Powers Resolution that gives Congress the right to direct the president to pull out even during the sixty-day period? Does it constitute, in effect, a legislative veto of his actions of the kind the Supreme Court held unconstitutional? Is the constitutional question here one that needs to be determined in the near term if we are to have an end to this debate?

REPRESENTATIVE CHENEY: I would like to relate an anecdote to the group on that point. I had the opportunity recently to travel in the Soviet Union. At one point I was pinned in an aircraft with two high Soviet officials who grilled me for three hours on the significance of the *Chadha* decision, which struck down the legislative veto, and what it meant for the implementation of the War Powers Resolution. Their conclusion after having studied it at least as closely as most American politicians was that indeed the president has far more authority and flexibility to commit troops in the future than he had in the past. I do not want to look to the Soviet Union for interpretation of our Constitution, but it is important and noteworthy that our primary adversary has good knowledge of that decision and interest in it. The decision that the Court handed down does not bode well for the legislative veto features of the War Powers Resolution, and the provision that would require the president to act by a simple majority vote of both houses of Congress is indeed a violation of separation of powers.

REPRESENTATIVE HAMILTON: I agree with Representative Cheney that the provision of the War Powers Resolution that permits the Congress to order the troops pulled out through a concurrent resolution is highly suspect in light of the Supreme Court decision. It is probably unconstitutional. There is a separability clause in the War Powers Resolution, however, and the balance of the resolution might still stand.

SENATOR MATHIAS: This anecdote of an experience on a Russian aircraft reminds me of a conversation with Marshal Ogarkov, a member of the Soviet armed forces. He was extremely interested in whether we were really going to dig 2,600 holes in the ground for the MX, as discussed during a previous incarnation of that debate. The interesting thing is how much high Soviet officials know about what is going on in America, and the depressing thing is how little high American officials know about what is going on in the Soviet Union. That is a point we ought to take to heart.

The question of the *Chadha* decision and whether the legislative veto is a problem does not affect a large part of the War Powers Resolution. The original statutory sixty-day limit on the use of troops overseas is not affected by the Supreme Court decision. That is untouched. The provisions on the growth of forces and the change of mission and the change of scope of the mission are untouched by the Supreme Court decision. It is just one rather narrow issue that is in question. Senator Javits, the author of the War Powers Resolution, feels very strongly that the original constitutional powers on which the resolution was founded are broad enough to raise the resolution and its legislative veto provision above the level of the *Chadha* decision, and I think that is at least an arguable case.

GENERAL SCOWCROFT: It seems to me that the legislative veto provision is only one of several items where the constitutionality of the resolution is at best dubious. It is quite clearly counter to the Constitution.

MR. DALY: Would you briefly review that decision for us, Senator?

SENATOR MATHIAS: It deals with the so-called legislative veto: Congress passes a statute and the president signs it, but the statute says that if the Congress does not like the way the executive is executing or applying it, one house of the Congress or, in some cases, both houses can pass a resolution without the president's signature that suspends that practice. In the *Chadha* decision the Court said we must follow the constitutional process of having legislation passed by both houses and signed by the president.

MR. DALY: It has been suggested that there should be an institutionalized mechanism for confrontation between the executive and the legislature, some supercommittee of the Congress as a counterpart to the National Security Council, which would serve as an information system for the Congress. Another suggestion is to have members of the Congress sit on the National Security Council. Do these approaches interest any of you?

REPRESENTATIVE CHENEY: There is obviously a need for consultation and notification. We will always have a debate over whether or not consultation was adequate. One of the difficulties the president has when he tries to consult with the Congress is that not everybody in the Congress agrees that he has consulted with the right people. Even though President Reagan, for example, talked with the majority and minority leaders of the Congress before the Grenada invasion, a number of people, including some of my colleagues, will still say that was inadequate consultation. There will always be a debate over whether it ought to be ten or fifteen or fifty members who are consulted and over who has the authority to speak for the Congress under those circumstances.

We also run into a problem with respect to covert operations. In 1975 Congress and its committees had gone along with covert operations in Angola, but once the operations became public, Congress headed for the hills and adopted the Clark amendment and shut them down. No matter what kind of mechanism we set up, whether it is an executive committee of the Congress or a more regularized institutional arrangement with the elected leaders of the Congress, we always come back to the fact that nobody can really commit the entire Congress. When the president consults with a group from Congress, he always runs the risk that, even though the leaders may sign off, the troops may not follow.

REPRESENTATIVE HAMILTON: As General Scowcroft and Representative Cheney both say, on the point of consultation, the resolution is not clear; it is ambiguous. Just what is consultation? I believe that whether

44

or not the resolution works depends less on its language than on the attitude with which the Congress and the executive branch approach it. If we have an attitude of mutual respect and good faith, this resolution will work. If we do not have that, it will not work, no matter what is written into it with regard to consultation. The issue is more one of respect and good faith between the two branches than of specific requirements about consultation. I have looked at some amendments spelling out more completely what consultation means; they may improve the resolution, although it is hard for me to see that they would improve it greatly.

MR. DALY: Would any of you look kindly on having members of Congress serve with the National Security Council?

SENATOR MATHIAS: I think that would cause real constitutional problems. We are committed to the philosophy of separation of powers, and I do not see how we could have that kind of overlap.

I do not find as much trouble with consultation. I think it was entirely proper for the president to call in the legislative leaders. The impropriety occurred not in the people who were chosen but in the fact that the president did not consult them. They were simply called to the Oval Office at 8:00 P.M. and told that the troops were under way and were going to hit the beach at 5:00 in the morning. That is not consultation. Of course, I have to admit that very often the process of consultation is frustrated within the Congress itself. I remember the late Senator John McClellan used to say, "They don't tell me secrets in order for me to tell them to somebody else." He used to do what Senator Hollings calls "squat on it." That of course does diffuse the value of consultation. What we need here is just common sense; when the majority leader of the Senate is told something, he knows the critical people who need that information, and he can share it with them. It will work if common sense prevails, but that seems to be in short supply.

REPRESENTATIVE CHENEY: Senator Mathias is trying to define what would have been acceptable in the case of Grenada, for example. We had a situation there in which the president believed American lives were at stake and the only way to rescue them was through his decision, within his prerogatives as commander in chief, to mount a military operation, where any prior notice might well have led to serious loss of life among civilians or military personnel. Under such circumstances, when the whole train of events lasts only a few days from the time the trouble arises until the action is taken, what is acceptable consultation?

SENATOR MATHIAS: I'll tell you exactly. There were critical decisions being made down on the golf course in Atlanta. If the president really wanted to have a consultation, he could have said, "Tip, come down here and play a round of golf with me," and the Speaker could have joined in those conversations. I think it comes back to Representative Hamilton's statement that it is the spirit in which consultation takes place that is important.

REPRESENTATIVE CHENEY: I was present the morning of the Grenada event when the president met with a larger group and with the bipartisan leadership at the White House. This was at the time the invasion was under way. Not one member of either party in the room, of some thirty members of the House and Senate, raised a question about the operation. But three days later the Speaker was publicly condemning the president for gunboat diplomacy. Ten days later, once he had all the facts, after he had sent a delegation down to look at what had happened in Grenada, he said, "Whoops, I was wrong; it was, indeed, a good operation." How does the president deal with that kind of situation if he is trying to use some kind of reasonable, rational decision-making process?

SENATOR MATHIAS: Let me give you a quick answer. He does not do it on the basis of one operation or one episode. There must be a continuous consulting climate in which there is an ability to exchange views, in which a member of Congress does not stand in awe of the president because he only sees him once in four years.

REPRESENTATIVE CHENEY: But isn't Grenada a classic example not of a decision to go to war but rather of a commander in chief's taking action to save American lives? Therefore, the War Powers Resolution should probably not apply at all.

REPRESENTATIVE HAMILTON: I don't think so. After all, we committed combat troops in a very major way; those combat troops met resistance; they were fired on and sustained casualties; we had people killed in war, in the invasion or rescue operation, whatever you want to call it. The fact that the American people and, I think, the Congress strongly supported the action is not the relevant point. There was a period when the president was in the process of deciding whether we should go into Grenada. If we had the right kind of spirit prevailing, the right kind of consultation would be to invite the congressional leadership in—and no member of Congress could complain if the leaders invited were of both parties and both houses of the Congress—and say, "This is what I am thinking about doing." The important point is prior consultation. In Grenada the order to invade had already been made; the president had signed that order before the 8:00 P.M. meeting. He did not call those leaders in to consult; he had already made up his mind to commit American troops for combat, and he did not consult with the leaders of Congress.

REPRESENTATIVE CHENEY: If he had consulted, what might have been the outcome?

REPRESENTATIVE HAMILTON: I don't know, but he has to give Congress the opportunity to be heard. These are tough questions. Maybe the question is not as tough in the Grenada situation as it would be in many others. The principle is that the most important decision government makes is whether or not to go to war. Should that decision be made by one person, or should it be made both by that person, the president, and by the Congress?

MR. DALY: During the debate about the division of war powers that began essentially in 1950 and ran through the 1960s and 1970s, there were people who disagreed strongly with the War Powers Resolution on the grounds that it gives the president powers that are not his under the Constitution. The thread ran continually through the debate that a War Powers Resolution meant to control the president does harm by giving him more powers than he has under the Constitution. Does that argument carry weight with you?

SENATOR MATHIAS: I don't think the War Powers Resolution alters the president's constitutional powers. They are what they are, and the War Powers Resolution does not change that. The argument you refer to is applied to the initial sixty-day period during which the president has an open license. Some people say that the Constitution does not give the president any days and therefore to say that a president can act during a sixty-day period without congressional authorization somehow enhances his power. I don't think it does. The sixty-day limit was a device built into the law in recognition of the kind of case where the president might have to act in an emergency to repel or to frustrate an invasion. The War Powers Resolution does not prevent the president from making foreign policy decisions. It simply says that they should be coordinated with the Congress, and under our system it is more efficient and effective to do that early.

GENERAL SCOWCROFT: I certainly agree that there should be consultation, and with the right spirit it can be worked out. The trouble is that with the right spirit we do not need the War Powers Resolution; with the wrong spirit, the War Powers Resolution does not really affect the executive. Suppose a president consults as broadly as you want and the verdict is that he should not do something. There is nothing that prevents him from going ahead and doing it.

SENATOR MATHIAS: True—for a while.

GENERAL SCOWCROFT: For a while. For that while there is another clear issue of constitutionality: If the role of commander in chief does not include the right to move troops around, it is absolutely meaningless. The Congress arrogates to itself the right to force the president by its inaction to do something the Constitution says he does not have to do, to pull the troops out. By its own inaction, not even by telling the president he should not continue the action for some reason but just because it is unable to make up its own mind, it forces the president to behave other than as the commander in chief.

REPRESENTATIVE HAMILTON: The war-making powers are clearly divided in the Constitution. It does not give all the power to the president or all the power to the Congress. It is a shared power, and that is all we are trying to say in the War Powers Resolution. When we make a decision to go to war, let us make sure it is a shared, collective judgment.

GENERAL SCOWCROFT: But it was shared before. Take the Cooper-Church amendments concerning Vietnam, to cut off our use of military forces in and over Cambodia and so on. There are many ways for the Congress to insert into legislation the restrictions they feel are important, and without an item veto the president is stuck with them.

SENATOR MATHIAS: General, let me present a hypothetical situation to you. Do you think that the power of the commander in chief is so broad that the president of the United States could direct naval vessels with marines aboard to sail into the Gulf of Finland and order them to land in Leningrad, regardless of the opposition they might face, without any authorization from the Congress?

GENERAL SCOWCROFT: I suspect he could, yes. And I think that is not very dissimilar to what President Jefferson did against the Barbary pirates.

SENATOR MATHIAS: Knowing that was going to provoke World War III, do you think that would be within the power of the president?

GENERAL SCOWCROFT: The president can do a number of things that could under some circumstances provoke World War III, but that is a bizarre, extreme example. I cannot conceive of any president that any of us have known contemplating anything like that.

SENATOR MATHIAS: In the twenty years I have been in the Congress, I have witnessed things that I could never have conceived of the day I arrived.

MR. DALY: We have covered this subject very broadly, and I think it is time for the question-and-answer session. May I have the first question, please?

ROBERT LOCKWOOD, Pentagon: My question is directed to Representative Hamilton, who has done much work on improving the process of consultation between the executive and legislative branches. In light of the background and material and information he has collected over the years, we could all benefit from his views on what is available to the president to conduct operations of humanitarian rescue such as the Grenada incident.

REPRESENTATIVE HAMILTON: The authority is not in the War Powers Resolution, although that has been one of the suggestions for an amendment to the act. It is broadly accepted that one of the powers that attend a commander in chief is to protect American citizens and to rescue them. So far as I know, the authority of a president to go into a Grenada situation to rescue Americans is simply an extension of his powers as commander in chief.

SENATOR MATHIAS: When we are talking about what authority the president has in such a situation, we ought also to look at what inhibitions there are to his authority. If I had been in the meeting that Representative Cheney described, I would certainly have asked a question about the inhibitions imposed by the Treaty of Rio—signed by members of the Organization of American States—in which there is a clear prohibition against intervention by force.

GENERAL SCOWCROFT: But don't you think those questions were raised in the debate within the executive branch?

SENATOR MATHIAS: I hope so, but I don't know.

GENERAL SCOWCROFT: I can assure you that they were and that such decisions are not made lightly. Anybody can profit by wider consultation, but to imagine that only one man is making a decision is really an exaggeration. The process involves the entire executive branch, which considers options and pros and cons; they might come up with the wrong answer, no question about that.

SENATOR MATHIAS: We are sure that was true when you were the president's national security adviser, but I would feel better if that consultation were repeated with the legislative branch.

REPRESENTATIVE CHENEY: There comes a time, doesn't there, Senator, when somebody has to make a decision? When Jimmy Carter was president, I was not very pleased with his style of operation or the quality of the decisions made in his administration. But for the time a president is the constitutional president of the United States, he has the authority to make those kinds of decisions and judgments on behalf of all of us. If he makes a mistake, obviously we may pay a price for it; but we have to trust him to make certain decisions. To keep coming back to the notion that every set of circumstances in which military force might be used lends itself to consultation and legal arguments is nice, but the world doesn't work that way.

WALTER MUTHER, Associated Industries of Massachusetts: Representative Hamilton, given the consequences of the War Powers Resolution as I hear it interpreted, we had better have pretty quick wars to avoid the problem that congressional inaction could bring them to an end in sixty days. It is very hard to understand how that would be implemented, but that is what you say it stands for. Is that correct?

REPRESENTATIVE HAMILTON: I would say that to sustain a war requires the support of the Congress and the American people. They ought to be in on the takeoff decision; if they are not, the chances of the president's being able to sustain the war are not good. That is all we are seeking to do—to bring the Congress into that decision-making process.

GENERAL SCOWCROFT: Are you arguing that the Congress and the American people were not in on the takeoff in Vietnam? As I review the debate over the Gulf of Tonkin resolution, it seems quite clear what the potential of U.S. involvement was.

REPRESENTATIVE HAMILTON: I don't think I even mentioned the Vietnam War.

50

GENERAL SCOWCROFT: No, but that seems to me the implication of what you are saying, that somehow things have to be clear and, if they are, Congress and the American people will not bail out if things do not go well.

REPRESENTATIVE HAMILTON: If I were in the executive branch and were making such a weighty decision as the commitment of troops, I would want to know that the leaders of the Congress were going to support me.

GENERAL SCOWCROFT: I agree completely.

REPRESENTATIVE HAMILTON: If that is your feeling, how would you carry it out? It seems to me that you would at least call the leadership in and go over the matter in some detail before a final decision to commit troops.

GENERAL SCOWCROFT: That depends on the circumstances.

REPRESENTATIVE HAMILTON: I can envision circumstances when it is not possible to do that.

MR. DALY: Former Senator Frank Church, who was chairman of the Foreign Relations Committee, voted for the War Powers Resolution in 1973, but he is having second thoughts. He said, "If the president uses the armed forces in action that is both swift and successful, then there is no reason to expect the Congress to do other than applaud. If the president employs forces in an action that is swift but *unsuccessful*, then the Congress is faced with a *fait accompli* and, although it may rebuke the president, it could do little else. If the action is a foreign war that is large and sustained, the argument that the War Powers Resolution forces the Congress to confront that decision overlooks the fact that it has no other course to take. The Congress must appropriate the money to make it possible for this sustained action to be sustained." So I wonder whether we have done very much to further our purpose through the War Powers Resolution.

SENATOR MATHIAS: I think Frank Church said nothing more than Representative Hamilton has said here. The question is whether the resolution can be effective in having the best judgments made in the affairs of the American people. We are groping for means and mechanisms for arriving at the very best judgments that are humanly possible. The War Powers Resolution is not holy writ; it is a means by which we reach out for a better way to make decisions. We have made some bloopers over the years, and we would like to reduce the incidence of mistakes. Whether the act will ultimately be effective will depend on how we use it. We are in an evolutionary period in which the president and the Congress are interpreting it, and we may, as a result of this exercise, come up with a better way of doing business. I hope we will. Perhaps each side will have to give a little and adjust a little, but that is the traditional way of improving the body politic.

JOHN RALM, Clackamas Community College, Oregon City, Oregon: My question is for Representative Cheney. If the Supreme Court were to declare the War Powers Resolution of 1973 unconstitutional because it infringes upon the president's power to commit troops, what legislative alternatives would you propose?

REPRESENTATIVE CHENEY: My view is that we do not need the War Powers Resolution. If the Court strikes it down, I expect it would be on the basis that it constitutes a legislative veto: The president does not have the opportunity to veto an act of the Congress directing him to withdraw troops; it therefore violates the separation of powers. The heart of having the relations between the president and the Congress work is basically a requirement of good faith effort on both sides. My view is that Congress already has adequate means to set restrictions and restraints, and it has powers and authority to intervene if the president does make a serious mistake. It has the power of the purse and the opportunity to hold hearings and conduct oversight investigations and decide whether Congress wants to sustain an effort after the fact. In the 1980s and beyond we are very unlikely to find ourselves in circumstances where the kind of conflict envisioned in the War Powers Resolution is likely to arise. Presidents have to be trusted to some extent. Once they are elected, we delegate enormous authority to them directly and indirectly. We build nuclear weapons systems and give them total control over those systems without consultation with the Congress. Having made that leap of faith, we can trust the president to be commander in chief. There is no need for a replacement for the War Powers Resolution if it should be struck down.

SENATOR MATHIAS: There is a subjective value to the War Powers Resolution that perhaps has not been sufficiently appreciated. During the debate in which it was first adopted, Senator Javits used to say that it was like a sign at a railroad crossing, that it was simply saying, stop, look, and listen before embarking on this journey overseas. That is the effect we hoped it would have on the executive branch. But there is an important subjective effect on the legislative branch. In a nonadversarial way, the act provides a framework for examining an operation. When I introduced the resolution, in 1969, to repeal the Gulf of Tonkin resolution—I finally took up Lyndon Johnson's challenge—that was an adversarial action. But the periodic reviews that are provided for in the War Powers Resolution do not have to be adversarial. People will take sides within the debate, but the existence of the debate itself becomes a matter of procedure and is neutral.

GENERAL SCOWCROFT: I suggest that is not the way it is viewed by the executive branch. It is viewed as an irritant and considered as showing congressional intent to infringe on the prerogatives of the president. It prevents the cooperative consultation that I think is the fundamental answer to the problem.

REPRESENTATIVE CHENEY: I don't think we can find an example in modern times when a president has failed to do what the War Powers Resolution expects him to do about consultation and notification. I don't know of anybody who has served in the presidency in the last thirty or forty or fifty years or longer who would have made a decision in a highhanded fashion to commit troops in a way that ultimately lacked the broad public support such a decision requires. Certainly that was not Lyndon Johnson's intention when he got involved in Southeast Asia. Certainly that was not the intention of Congress when they supported that involvement. In the end public opinion swung against our involvement after years of developments and gradual, constant escalation, but nothing in the War Powers Resolution would have changed that. I think we do have to rely to some extent on good faith interpretation of our responsibilities both as legislators and as executives, and I think that has been there in virtually every case.

REPRESENTATIVE HAMILTON: Let me make an observation about the War Powers Resolution from the standpoint of the Congress. General Scowcroft talked about it from the standpoint of the executive branch, and I think his observation was accurate and correct.

From the standpoint of the Congress, it seems to me, the War Powers Resolution has had great symbolic importance as a reassertion of congressional authority. Those of us who served in the Congress right after Vietnam came out of that experience with a strong feeling that we had not done our job very well. The country had made a major decision that had not worked out well, and we were criticized very strongly. The War Powers Resolution grew out of that experience, and it passed the House and the Senate overwhelmingly. It was passed strongly over a presidential veto. It became very important for us symbolically.

The second thing I can say about it from the standpoint of the Congress is that it forces Congress to face the tough questions, such as, Are you going to leave the marines in Lebanon or not? Congress likes to duck tough questions; so maybe one beneficial aspect of this resolution is that it does make the Congress confront tough questions that it might otherwise avoid.

GENERAL SCOWCROFT: I agree with that except for the provision whereby it does allow the Congress to duck the question. By its inaction it forces the president to do something.

SENATOR MATHIAS: One of the reasons we are meeting is to discuss constitutionality; therefore, I drag you back to the history of the Constitution. The executive side of this argument is presented as the need to repose confidence in the judgment of the president and his advisers. Alexander Hamilton was never thought to be soft on the executive. He was always viewed as an advocate of a strong executive. In *The Federalist Papers,* however, he wrote, "The history of human conduct does not warrant that exalted opinion of human virtue which would make it wise in a nation to commit interests of so delicate and momentous a kind as those which concern intercourse with the rest of the world to the sole disposal of a magistrate created in circumstance as would be the President of the United States." There was a kind of concern expressed at the very birth of the republic that reflects the problems we are discussing here.

GENERAL SCOWCROFT: I agree with that, but to imagine that the world was so different that the framers did not know what they were doing is wrong. A recent study found that about 10 percent of the military engagements throughout the world between 1780 and 1880 were consequent to a declaration of war. So the idea that undeclared wars are a recent phenomenon—

SENATOR MATHIAS: The degree is different, but the circumstances are pretty standard.

GENERAL SCOWCROFT: In the process of writing the Constitution, the words "make war" were deliberately changed to "declare war." That cannot have been accidental, and that is a very important change. One is recognizing a situation; the other is initiating a situation.

SENATOR MATHIAS: But Hamilton, who was there, argues that the power was not vested solely in the president and should not have been.

GENERAL SCOWCROFT: And it is not, because the Congress raises and maintains armies.

ROBERT GOLDWIN, director of Constitutional Studies, American Enterprise Institute: Senator Mathias, the passage from Alexander Hamilton that you quoted was in reference not to making war or declaring war but to the Senate's power of constitutional "advice and consent" on treaties and appointments. That raises an interesting question related to what Representative Hamilton was saying about bringing Congress into decision making. Do you mean there should be congressional "consent" in the same sense as "advice and consent" with regard to treaties? That is, if you restrict the power of the president to the extent that he must consult with members of Congress, and they give him opposing or conflicting advice, what should the president do? Do you really mean that congressmen should have some part of the decision-making power? Wouldn't that put in real question the whole principle of separation of powers?

SENATOR MATHIAS: I think we made that clear in reference to the question about whether legislators should serve on the National Security Council. I think that clearly would be a violation of the separation of powers and under the American Constitution would not be proper. I am not suggesting that. I think what Hamilton was looking at was foreign policy, and war is, of course, the ultimate act of foreign policy. So I think war powers are clearly comprehended in his thinking. A coordinate decision must be made. I do not see how we can ever embody in a statute precisely how this will occur. Lee Hamilton has one kind of personality, and Dick Cheney has another; there will be presidents with whom one of them will be sympathetic and the other will not. General Scowcroft and Dick Cheney, both having served in the highest positions in the White House, know how personalities become important in policy making and execution, and that is one reason that it is impossible to create an absolutely rigid system of consultation, that from administration to administration it will change. But the president must be exposed to all the considerations *before* he makes a decision.

REPRESENTATIVE HAMILTON: You asked whether the Congress should consent—why shouldn't the Congress consent? What is wrong in a democracy about making a judgment in a democratic manner? That is all we are asking.

GENERAL SCOWCROFT: Should consent be mandatory? Should it be binding on the president?

REPRESENTATIVE HAMILTON: The question was whether the Congress should consent to the decision, and I see nothing wrong with that. What kind of a war can the president of the United States carry out if the Congress of the United States does not consent?

REPRESENTATIVE CHENEY: In many respects we have already given prior approval. We have appropriated the funds and raised the army and purchased the equipment and built the missiles and the bombers, and the president has the authority to make decisions about how to use those things. To suggest that the president can involve the Congress as deeply as I think you would like to in advance of the actual commitment of troops strikes me as not very practical.

SENATOR MATHIAS: I simply do not believe that the existence of the defense establishment is in some way an authorization to the president to start out on foreign adventures.

REPRESENTATIVE CHENEY: It is a recognition that we live in a dangerous and hostile world and from time to time may have to defend ourselves and our interests. We look to the president to make decisions that are naturally made by a commander in chief rather than a legislative body.

SENATOR MATHIAS: We entrust that final decision to the president, but we have confidence that the secretary of state and the secretary of defense will have some comment, that the Joint Chiefs of Staff will talk about the military feasibility, that the Central Intelligence Agency will provide basic information, that the whole apparatus of government will be brought to bear. At some point in that decision-making process—and I certainly did not mean to imply that this was something the president decides in the shower on his own—there is room and time to register the congressional point of view.

REPRESENTATIVE HAMILTON: We have to draw a distinction between two situations. One is an emergency. Representative Cheney, you refer to that frequently, and I think you are probably correct. There are going to be times when the president has to act. Do you believe that was true in Grenada, that American citizens had to be rescued right then, and the president really did not have time? I can see how you can make a case for the president moving very quickly. But that is not the only situation in which a president will be confronted with a decision to commit troops. Should we invade Nicaragua today? That is a possible question on the agenda of the country. If I were a president reflecting on that question today, I would call Senator Mathias and others and talk with them about it. That is what we are saying, and that kind of situation is very different from an emergency.

GENERAL SCOWCROFT: The War Powers Resolution does not say that the president will not attack this or that or the other. It says the president may not move troops, may not introduce troops in certain areas. That brings us back to Representative Cheney's point about having raised armies: What can the president do with them? If the commander in chief cannot deploy and move his forces around, the term "commander in chief" is absolutely meaningless. We are not talking about specifically going to war; there is nothing about that in the War Powers Resolution.

SENATOR MATHIAS: We are talking about hostilities, and that *is* in the War Powers Resolution.

GENERAL SCOWCROFT: Where it is possible. We are not talking about the president using forces offensively to attack.

TERRY EMERSON, office of Senator Barry Goldwater: I have a quick comment on Alexander Hamilton. In a famous set of written debates with James Madison, Hamilton made a clear distinction between offensive and defensive war. He said the Congress can commence offensive war through the declaration power but the president possesses the power to initiate defensive actions on behalf of the United States.

My question to the panel is whether any member would wish to test the War Powers Resolution against the history immediately preceding World War II. Take the actions of President Franklin Roosevelt in 1941. In 1940 Congress had renewed the military draft by a single vote. Yet in 1941, before any declaration of war, Roosevelt sent American marines equipped for combat to both Greenland and Iceland. He gave them orders to cooperate fully with British armed forces already there defending the islands against Nazi Germany. Roosevelt also ordered the American navy to escort British shipping in the North Atlantic and to shoot on sight German U-boats. All this before any declaration of war. Under the War Powers Resolution, Congress would have had to vote within sixty days on whether to extend President Roosevelt's powers. I ask whether the War Powers Resolution in that situation would not have led to a total disaster for the democracies of the world through an isolationist Congress's refusing to ratify President Roosevelt's wise actions.

REPRESENTATIVE CHENEY: The gentleman stated the case eloquently; I think he is absolutely right.

SENATOR MATHIAS: We can make only a hypothetical judgment about what might have happened if the War Powers Resolution had been in effect. It is difficult to say, given the unpredictability of history. Senator Goldwater, for example, voted against the War Powers Resolution but thereafter called for the immediate withdrawal of the marines from Lebanon. I don't know what real conclusions we can draw.

MR. DALY: This concludes another public policy forum presented by the American Enterprise Institute for Public Policy Research. On behalf of AEI, our hearty thanks to the distinguished and expert panelists, Representative Lee H. Hamilton, Senator Charles McC. Mathias, Jr., Representative Dick Cheney, and Lieutenant General Brent Scowcroft, and our thanks also to our guests and experts in the audience for their participation.

Appendix

Gerald R. Ford

Questions of war and peace, which are the responsibility of the president in the White House and of the Congress are too serious not to be of dual responsibility. From my practical experience in the Congress for twenty-five years and two and a half years in the White House, however, I thoroughly believe that trying to put on paper a precise procedure by which things have to be done in a crisis is impractical in the first place. Second, I believe it is unconstitutional since it undercuts a president's responsibility as commander in chief of our military forces. And third, the most important point, a president of the United States, under any and all circumstances, has to maximize his effort either to maintain the peace or, where there is no peace, to obtain it. I firmly believe, as a practical matter, that the War Powers Resolution with all its requirements handicaps a president in trying to achieve and maintain the peace.

Now let me take a specific example of what happened under the War Powers Resolution during my administration. I am sure people recall the seizure of the merchant vessel *Mayaguez* in 1975, when the Cambodians violated international law by seizing an American ship off the shores of Cambodia. That precipitated, of course, a challenge to my administration as to how we could get the crew back without any loss of life and how we could recover the ship itself. Under the War Powers Resolution, we would have been handicapped in trying to go through all of the procedures that were required. We had to take action, and we did; and the result was that the crew and ship were recovered from the enemy.

Now, that did not mean that we failed to consult with the Congress; we invited as many key congressmen and senators as we could find to the Cabinet Room. We informed them of the facts, and we outlined what we were going to do, which later turned out to be successful. But

NOTE: President Ford's comments were videotaped on December 7, 1983, and have been edited.

if we had been required to do this in a straight-jacketed way, we would have lost valuable time, we might not have been able to move as promptly and precisely as we did, and the crew of the *Mayaguez* might have suffered the same fate as the crew of the *Pueblo*, the American ship and crew seized by the North Koreans and held for some eighteen months. I was determined to avoid the *Pueblo* situation developing under any circumstances, so we moved rapidly. We consulted with the Congress, but we never conceded that the War Powers Resolution was applicable. If we had, we might have been delayed, we might have been hamstrung, and we might not have been successful.

I had my chief of congressional liaison with the Congress, Jack Marsh, and his assistants notify the congressional leadership, Democratic as well as Republican, that an American ship had been illegally seized. I also indicated some of the options we faced. We then invited the leadership of the House and Senate, Democrats as well as Republicans, to the White House for a meeting in the Cabinet Room where we had in attendance the secretaries of defense and state, the chairman of the joint chiefs of staff, and the director of the Central Intelligence Agency. A full briefing was presented. We went through the process of notification and giving information, but we did not concede that what we did was covered by the War Powers Resolution.

We made our decision based on what we felt was requisite military action and appropriate diplomatic action, since we were operating through diplomatic as well as military channels. The views of various congressional members were not based on the kind of indepth information that a president gets from his staff. Members of Congress have many other duties. Their principal responsibility is not to be commander in chief. Information as to what is transpiring during a crisis on a minute-by-minute or hour-by-hour basis, therefore, is not available to them.

A president, on the other hand, where the Constitution gives him the responsibility as commander in chief, has to know by the hour what's happening so that he can act in a responsible manner. You cannot have 535 commanders in chief. You cannot have 535 secretaries of state. Their duties, under our constitution are different—important but different, from the president's.

It is more difficult to bring the Congress into decision making during an emergency than it is on broader strategy, for example in planning a position for our government on a strategic arms limitation agreement. In the latter case, we have time. World events or tragedies do not always happen during the working hours of the Congress, even when Congress is in session, so you cannot write a textbook on how consultation should take place. A president ought to maximize his efforts to notify and to consult the Congress, but he cannot give away his responsibility as commander in chief when the lives of American military personnel are involved.

Because it controls the purse strings, the Congress can always limit executive actions by an amendment which would say, "None of the funds appropriated herein or none of the funds authorized herein can be expended for this particular military operation." That is the way Congress can exercise control any day it is in session and that is the appropriate way under our Constitution.

3

The Constitution and the Budget Process

Dick Cheney
John Charles Daly
James C. Miller III
Norman Ornstein
Leon E. Panetta

J OHN CHARLES DALY, former ABC News chief: This public policy forum, one of a series presented by the American Enterprise Institute, will examine the constitutional division of responsibility between the president and the Congress for formulating and implementing a federal budget. Our subject: The Constitution and the Budget Process.

As the new 99th Congress settled down in early 1985, more than three dozen acts and resolutions sought reform of the budget process, or of the relationship between the legislative and executive departments in its implementation. Some sought constitutional amendment, others basic reforms in the congressionally mandated form, content, and rules that govern the process.

The Constitution, as many of you know from civics class in high school, stipulates that Congress shall have the power to lay and collect taxes, duties, imposts, and excises; to pay the debt and provide for the common defense and general welfare of the United States; to borrow money on the credit of the United States; and to coin money and regulate its value.

The Constitution also says that all bills for raising revenue shall originate in the House of Representatives and that, of course, all legislation, including economic matters, must be approved by both houses of the Congress and signed by the president to become the law of the land.

In the now-historic tradition of checks and balances in our constitutional system, the president has a qualified veto over legislation, and a two-thirds vote of both houses of the Congress is required to override it. The Founding Fathers, however, said nothing about whether the veto power might be applied to part of a bill, or could be applied only to an entire bill.

That distinction looms large in budget reform debates today, and has for over 100 years. In 1876, for instance, President Grant signed a river and harbor bill, always a notorious repository of pork barrel items for individual congressmen.

Claiming discretionary authority, Grant announced bluntly that none of the money would be expended for "works of purely private or local interest." This impoundment of appropriated funds—really a euphemism for a line-item veto, and one not even exposed to override—brought no real objection from the Congress for nearly a century.

It was used sparingly, except in wartime emergency by President Franklin Roosevelt. Congress, however, finally struck back in 1974, as part of a critical reexamination of the budget process, which had been undergoing modernization since the end of World War I.

Now, to examine this modernization, to measure its effectiveness, and to consider what still needs to be done, we have a distinguished and expert panel. Representative Dick Cheney, Republican of Wyoming, served in the Ford administration, first as deputy assistant to the president, then as assistant to the president and White House chief of staff. He was first elected to the Congress in 1978. He is chairman of the House Republican Policy Committee and a member of the House Committee on Interior and Insular Affairs.

Dr. James C. Miller III, director of the Office of Management and Budget, was chairman of the Federal Trade Commission and an AEI resident scholar and co-director of the American Enterprise Institute's Center for the Study of Government Regulation.

Representative Leon E. Panetta, Democrat from California's 16th District, served for six years on the House Budget Committee. He was a leading participant in the budget-making process during President Reagan's first term, and he served as the chairman of the Budget Committee's Task Force on Reconciliation.

Dr. Norman Ornstein, resident scholar of the American Enterprise Institute and a visiting professor of political science at Johns Hopkins University, is the author of, among other books, *The New Congress* and *Vital Statistics on Congress*.

The modern era in the budget process really began in 1921 with the Budget and Accounting Act, described as a turning point in executive/legislative budget relations. The act required the president to prepare an executive budget for submission to the Congress at the beginning of each session, established a Bureau of the Budget to help the president prepare his budget, and created the General Accounting Office—the GAO—independent of the executive department, to keep an eye on executive agency expenditures and to provide information for congressional review of the budget.

During the 1940s, 1950s, and 1960s, further refinement and modification sought more efficient and effective budget methods, among them a mandated legislative budget to be drawn up each year by

February 15, to cover two years, and a single omnibus appropriation bill, covering one year.

With all the earnest effort and thrashing about, nonetheless, the budget process lacked cohesion and efficiency. Budget details took up a disproportionate amount of time and produced unsatisfactory results at a time when economic questions played an increasingly vital role in virtually all domestic and foreign affairs decisions.

Finally, in 1974, President Nixon's impoundment of some $18 billion already appropriated in congressional spending bills triggered the Congressional Budget and Impounding Control Act. The act overhauled the budget process, created budget committees in both houses of the Congress, established a Congressional Budget Office, and set a timetable for matching appropriations and authorizations to binding limits on spending totals.

The final title of that act, by the way, took care of presidential impoundments: whether rescissions or deferrals, Congress would have the final authority on all impoundments.

Now, more than a decade later, the 1974 act has been found wanting by many who have participated in the budget process in the Senate and the House, and by those who have observed there the deficits, the huge public debt, and the chaotic efforts to establish viable and effective spending priorities.

So what can be done? Gentlemen, I would pose the same question to each of you in turn: After ten years of trial and testing, and keeping constitutional provisions in mind, does the history of the 1974 Budget Act give us any hope of addressing our chronic failure to manage prudently public spending and revenue raising, as we expect every element of the private sector, down to the family unit, to do?

JAMES C. MILLER III, director, Office of Management and Budget: I believe that there is some hope, but that hope is evaporating fast. We have had some successes with the Budget Act. The Congressional Budget Office's resources have been valuable to congressmen and senators. But resources between appropriations accounts have not been traded off as advertised. And even with an additional three months, not a single appropriations bill was ready for the president's signature by the beginning of the fiscal year.

Finally, let me say that the budget deficit has grown by leaps and bounds, so that control over the budget process is, I think, in some doubt.

LEON E. PANETTA, U.S. representative (Democrat, California): What has been seen over the years is that while we can put a process in place, process alone is not the answer in dealing with budget issues. We still need the courage and the leadership to make tough choices.

The problem with the budget process put in place in 1974 is that it worked relatively well when the choices were relatively easy. But now, when we have to either cut defense, raise taxes, or cut cost of living indexes for social security recipients, the process bogs down.

We can put in place any kind of process we want, but without the courage to make tough choices and without leadership, from the president as well as the Congress, the deficit continues to go up.

RICHARD B. CHENEY, U.S. representative (Republican, Wyoming): I would concur with Mr. Panetta's judgment. What we have learned is that the 1974 act has not worked for many of the reasons Jim Miller cites. Any statutory budget process ultimately requires the creation of working majorities on the House and the Senate floors to implement it. Without those majorities, without the consensus among members of at least 50 percent plus one, no statutory process appears to solve the problem.

The current frustration with the process is so great that it has led to efforts like the Gramm-Rudman proposal, to make cuts automatic. It has also led to a debate about whether or not we ought to amend the Constitution and thereby fundamentally change authorities over the budget, so that we can deal with the problem.

NORMAN J. ORNSTEIN, AEI resident scholar: The current budget mechanism is clearly an improvement over what existed before. The process works better than it would if we did not have such a mechanism in place now. My colleagues are absolutely right: the problem is not the process. It is, however, a natural American inclination to consider changing the process or to tinker with it if we have a more fundamental difficulty.

The fundamental difficulty here is not just a lack of leadership or a lack of consensus among the elites about priorities; it is also a lack of public consensus as to what the problem is, much less what our priorities ought to be. And ours is a system designed not to act, not to take drastic steps, unless we have such a consensus. We have to find a way to develop that consensus, not just tinker with the process.

MR. DALY: There have been two main approaches to dealing with our budget problem. One would limit the size and growth of the federal budget by constitutional amendment; the other would change and try to improve existing law by revising congressional procedures in the budget process. The Gramm-Rudman-Hollings bill has already been mentioned. It requires a balanced budget by 1991, and would reach it through automatic reductions of major elements of the budget, if the deficit exceeds the annual targets. Dr. Miller, the president endorsed that bill. Did he have reservations?

DR. MILLER: The president is very concerned about the overall level of the deficit. He believes it important to get it back down, and believes that the Gramm-Rudman theory of action-forcing events is the way to go.

He thinks that we still spend too much on many domestic programs. There is still a lot of pork that needs to be taken away. There are programs that do not benefit the vast majority of taxpayers—they benefit instead special interests—and those ought to be taken away.

I know it is very difficult for elected officials to come to Congress and not bring home the pork. It is even more difficult for them to come to Congress and lose the pork that they have. It is therefore extraordinarily difficult to develop a social compact in which congressmen and senators will all agree to reduce levels of spending. No one wants to give up his piece of pork unless everyone else is giving up theirs.

The advantage of the Gramm-Rudman-Hollings approach is that it forces a social compact among congressmen and senators and with the president of the United States, which would lead to a lower budget deficit.

REPRESENTATIVE CHENEY: With all due respect—and I am a Republican and a strong supporter of Ronald Reagan—I take offense at the notion that somehow all congressmen are concerned only about pork, or that they are unwilling to make those difficult decisions and to cast those tough votes.

Although I've agreed with the president's spending priorities, there is a fundamental difference of opinion in the country at large, reflected in divisions within the Congress, between the two parties, between both houses, and between Congress and the president, over what those priorities ought to be.

And as much as I like, admire, and respect Ronald Reagan, the fact is that, when it was time to put together a budget package in the Congress, the president took defense off the table, saying, "That is not an item. We are not going to cut defense." The Democrats in the Congress take the domestic programs off the table. "We are not going to cut those." Both parties run to see who can be first to take social security off the table. "We are not going to cut that." Then the president says, "We cannot raise taxes," and the Democrats agree

69

with that. So all that is left to negotiate over is the deficit, and it gets bigger and bigger and bigger.

Many of us have strong feelings about the programs and the directions of the priorities that we think ought to be established. But I would not want to leave people with the view that somehow Congress cares about "pork" and the president alone cares about fiscal responsibility.

DR. MILLER: There are obviously many things to consider and there are some different priorities. But we went through an election in 1984 in which the president carried all states but one, and questions about tax increases, for example, arguably were settled there. There is a perception among the public, and the polls tend to show it, that there is a need to deal with the budget deficit, but there is no enthusiasm for doing so by increasing taxes. And so it seems to me we have to do it by reducing spending.

REPRESENTATIVE PANETTA: I do not think we can reach $200 billion deficits and not have everybody share the blame, whether it is Republican administrations or Democratic administrations or, for that matter, the House, Senate, and the president. We just do not get to that number unless all parties are somewhat responsible, because of their particular sets of priorities.

In trying to deal with a deficit that size, however, we have to look at the nature of the budget we are dealing with. Eighty-five percent of the federal budget, which now is around a trillion dollars, goes basically to three areas. Fifteen percent goes to interest payments on the debt, which is one of the fastest growing areas of the federal budget; about 45 percent goes to entitlement programs, largely retirement and pension programs, along with agricultural programs; and now close to 30 percent is going to defense spending. We could shut off the rest of the federal government's spending, and we would still run deficits of almost $150, $160 billion.

So the problem is that we have to address three areas: defense, entitlements, and revenues. If we do not put that kind of package together, we are never going to accomplish anything on the deficit.

But everybody is bogged down on that issue: the president has not moved on taxes or defense; Democrats in Congress have not moved on entitlements; and so the deficit goes up. That is the core of the problem that we are facing.

DR. ORNSTEIN: This is a problem that goes beyond the question of pork in many other ways. The president does not consider defense to be pork. Obviously, he wants a sizable spending increase here, and for some very good reasons.

There are not very many Americans who would consider most of those entitlement programs—which are direct benefit payments to individuals—pork. We do not think of social security as pork; we do not think of Medicare as pork; we do not think of veterans' pensions or veterans' health benefits as pork.

Interest on the debt, obviously, is off the table. So what is left? As Congressman Panetta suggested, about 15 percent of the budget. Now, that includes the FBI. Is that pork? Most people would not consider that to be pork. Medicaid or food stamps? Some might, but, after all, they are not very large items and wouldn't solve the deficit problem.

When we get down to what is commonly accepted as pork, which gets so much attention, it has gone down so sharply in real terms in the past several years that very little is left. Meanwhile the other items have gone up sharply.

We could eliminate every dam, every bridge, every river and harbor project—every one of those items that would meet the common definition of pork—and we would still have a deficit that is staggering by historical standards.

It is not a question of simply getting rid of things that people consider either pork or waste, or fraud and abuse, by common definition. Tough decisions must be made, without any consensus on priorities. Finally, we have to realize that the public out there believes, among other things, that it is morning in America, and that things are going very well, thank you. If we are talking about making decisions that are extremely tough—not just getting rid of waste, fraud, and pork—the public is not in the mood at this point to take that kind of enormous pain. And the political institutions set up by the Founding Fathers do not encourage politicians—no matter how courageous—to make tough decisions that bring enormous pain to large numbers of people if they are out of the mood to accept that pain except under extraordinary circumstances.

MR. DALY: We should address the fundamental issue of whether the necessary corrections in the process can be achieved only by amendment of the Constitution of the United States.

Do you feel we should pass a constitutional amendment making a balanced budget mandatory?

REPRESENTATIVE CHENEY: I have reached this point reluctantly, but it appears to me that we have to change the presumption of the process and make it more difficult for our political institutions—the president and the Congress—to spend more than we take in. How do we do that? I am prepared to support a constitutional amendment that would, in fact, make it more difficult to spend money. Some people talk about requiring a balanced budget. That has a nice ring to it. Realistically, though, that would be extremely hard to implement.

We could amend the Constitution to say we have to have at least a 60 or 65 percent majority in both houses of Congress to approve a deficit. We should make it the kind of extraordinary step that it is, the kind of important policy decision that now requires a two-thirds majority to ratify a Senate treaty, for example.

DR. MILLER: But Dick, that is exactly what I meant when I was talking about pork. It is very difficult for congressmen and senators to resist those pressures from back home to spend more.

REPRESENTATIVE CHENEY: A number of us in the House, Republicans specifically and some Democrats, have voted more often to cut the budget than Ronald Reagan has. We have often taken a more conservative stance on spending than the president has. It is not just a matter of members of Congress responding to back-home pressures. The pressures I feel and care about and try to respond to include cutting the budget, and we do it time after time. But whatever the process, whether constitutional amendment or Gramm-Rudman or any other alternative, the bottom line is that the president will have to make some tough decisions too. One of the features of Gramm-Rudman is that the president, in effect, has to decide between defense, entitlements, and taxes, because the deficit option is eliminated. The same is true of a constitutional amendment requiring a balanced budget.

If we eliminate the deficit as an option, then we have to decide what to do on entitlements, what to do on defense, and what to do on revenues.

DR. MILLER: For the reasons we have both described, there is an institutional bias to be corrected, and Gramm-Rudman-Hollings is an institutional way of correcting that bias. It forces the Congress and the president—

REPRESENTATIVE CHENEY: And the president. All right.

DR. MILLER: Yes—and the president, to make those tough choices. A balanced budget amendment to the Constitution—the kind we were talking about, where a super-majority of Congress would be required to approve spending beyond revenues taken in—is a similar institutional approach.

REPRESENTATIVE CHENEY: For a long time, it would ensure a correction of the present institutional bias.

REPRESENTATIVE PANETTA: But in either event I think Gramm-Rudman is in fact a crude tool. It was born in frustration over the failure to deal with the issues.

Anyone who has dealt with the budget knows that an across-the-board approach is not a careful one. Some priorities demand more spending, and some areas demand less. Across-the-board cuts are not responsible. Such legislation is a club to force the institution to do what it ought to be doing willingly.

The problem is that our forefathers really intended that we, as representatives, be accountable to the public. If we are not reducing the deficit, then, by God, the public ought to vote us, including the president, out of office. But if the public continues to support the programs that Congress and the president support, then every amendment in the world will not change much.

I am concerned about the arguments over a balanced-budget amendment. They convey the impression that simply enacting this process will solve our problems. I fear that this process can be as abused as much as the present budget process. Under a balanced-budget amendment, we can take things off budget. There is a move now, for instance, to take social security off budget. There will be a move to take defense off budget. We took the Strategic Petroleum Reserve off budget.

So there will be an effort to reduce the area we are dealing with. We will not have resolved the deficit issue—we will just have played shadow games.

DR. ORNSTEIN: We have gotten quickly to some fundamentals here that are worth pursuing. One is the question of whether there is, in fact, the deep institutional bias that Jim Miller suggested. I know Jim relies, to a degree, on the public choice literature, which is full of formal models suggesting a tremendous internal bias in Congress to spend on concrete projects of benefit only to individuals. Those models thus imply a bias on the part of democratic polities to spend, spend, spend.

I would argue that such a bias is, in fact, not there. For 180 years, we have had fundamentally the same institutions as today, and by and large—with the exception of the major wars—we had a budget that was pretty close to being in balance. We had many, many years of surpluses, along with years, unavoidably, of deep deficits, but overall, we were close to being in balance. The problem has only arisen in the past twenty years.

DR. MILLER: Right.

DR. ORNSTEIN: Now I am not sure there has been a structural change in the past twenty years that has somehow brought about our current deficit. Moreover, that literature suggests dramatic built-in increases in spending in precisely those areas that have gone down in the past twenty years. They have gone down in real terms, and they have gone down dramatically as a portion of the budget. The areas that have gone up are those that congressmen cannot claim credit for. They cannot say, "I take credit for the automatic cost of living adjustment you get in your social security."

Why did Congress insulate those areas? Congress enacted automatic cost-of-living adjustments in social security and in other entitlement programs precisely to keep spending down. We were getting, in a year-by-year process, increases in cost-of-living adjustments that were well beyond inflation. They had all the right motives for indexation.

That raises a second question. Indexation was a reform enacted for all the right reasons, but of course, reforms inevitably fall under the iron law of unintended consequences. Nobody anticipated the inflation we had in the 1970s, which tremendously increased those entitlement costs—in fact, it made them about 40 percent of the budget.

When we talk about structural changes such as the constitutional amendment Dick Cheney has suggested, which would retard spending by requiring a super majority, I can barely begin to think of all the unintended consequences. Minorities in Congress, for instance, could use this as a lever. With a third of the membership, they could bring the country to a halt in order to meet a whole series of objectives they might want. I can think of millions of unintended consequences that will result from a crude tool like Gramm-Rudman. It makes me think long and hard about undertaking a structural solution to what is not fundamentally, in my view, a structural problem.

MR. DALY: Isn't there a law on the books now saying that beginning in 1981 government budget outlays shall not exceed receipts?

REPRESENTATIVE CHENEY: Senator Byrd offered such an amendment back in the late 1970s, but there is no enforcement mechanism, so it is very easily gotten around.

Gramm-Rudman differs from that amendment in the sense that it tries to reform the basic Budget Act of 1974, and it provides an enforcement mechanism. If the president and Congress cannot agree on a budget that hits the legislated target, then we get sequestration and the automatic, across-the-board reductions that everybody admits is a crude tool.

I would like to ask this question: if we do not try procedural changes or constitutional changes, then what is the solution to the problem?

REPRESENTATIVE PANETTA: Let me give you a political answer, because I think that is where we have to look. Everybody understands that, to deal with a deficit the size of ours, we have to put pressure on the president, the Speaker, and the majority leader of the Senate to act on the areas of defense, entitlements, and taxes. That is the name of the game in our process. That is where leadership and courage would be involved—to come up with that kind of solution, not to hide in the trenches.

Everybody is playing chicken on this issue and that is a basic problem.

But what do we do instead? Rather than saying to the president and to the leadership, "You have to try to resolve the issue," we come up with a process solution that is simply a club to force the president to do what he should be doing anyway.

MR. DALY: How much support has Representative James Jones's suggestion of an economic summit had?

REPRESENTATIVE PANETTA: I think it makes a great deal of sense. That is what we ought to be pushing as a common-sense approach to this, not a process that may force a whole set of unintended consequences. That is why people elect representatives to office, to come up with those kinds of answers. We come up with them in the event of war and other crises. Now we have a budget crisis on our hands. It is time for urgent action at a leadership level.

REPRESENTATIVE CHENEY: But the summit idea is not a new suggestion. We have had the Group of 17, we have had the Rose Garden Agreements. I cannot even count all the agreements we have had in recent years. We do exactly as you say. We get the Speaker or his representatives, the president or his representatives in the room, and sit down and talk. Sometimes the meetings go on endlessly.

They have been at Jim Baker's house in the middle of the night; they have been in the White House and in Blair House, and all over town—nothing but meetings. When we are all through, the deficit still goes up. Nobody is going to touch entitlements; the Democrats get what they want on domestic spending; the president gets what he wants on defense; and so the numbers add to a $200 billion deficit.

And then we say, "Oh well, next year we will do better."

Maybe through a constitutional amendment, or through Gramm-Rudman if by no other means, we can take the deficit off the table and say, "Hey, guys, that is not negotiable anymore. Sit down and talk. We want an agreement. We want a summit accord of some kind. But we are not allowed anymore to do what we have done in the past, which is to say, 'Well, we will just take it out of the deficit.' "

DR. MILLER: I think right now we have two theories to explain a malady. One is that we have the wrong people in office, or that the people there are not strong enough to make the tough choices. The other is an institutional bias theory. And I tend toward the institutional bias idea. After all, if the institutions are neutral with respect to deficits, how can we explain the fact that for twenty-four of the last twenty-five years, we have experienced deficits?

I do not think every year we have had the wrong kind of people. We have had a lot of different presidents in the past twenty-five years, a lot of different members of Congress, and a lot of different members of the Senate. Yet we have run a deficit twenty-four of the last twenty-five years.

DR. ORNSTEIN: I do not think it is an institutional phenomenon. We have run deficits, as many other Western democracies have, in part because our norms have changed. Maybe it is because of modern economics; maybe it is a whole set of other reasons. But we went through a period when deficits were not considered as bad as in the nineteenth century.

We are also paying a price for bad decisions made in the 1960s, when we thought we could have both guns and butter. Some of it is a result of wrong decisions made for the right reasons—like the indexing of entitlements, perhaps.

Many of the solutions that are proposed, constitutional ones in particular, suggest it is only the people in Congress who have a spending bias. So let's give more power to the president. Let's give him the line-item veto. Let's give him more authority.

But when I look at other Western democracies, particularly parliamentary systems, with enormous authority in the executive, I see a much worse spending bias. Process solutions say essentially that we have tried everything else, so now let's try suicide.

REPRESENTATIVE CHENEY: A line-item veto is not a radical idea; forty-three out of the fifty governors do, in fact, have that authority today. Why not give it to the president?

REPRESENTATIVE PANETTA: But a line-item veto would apply to only about 15 percent of the federal budget.

REPRESENTATIVE CHENEY: It would apply to the defense budget as well.

REPRESENTATIVE PANETTA: But a large part of the defense budget, such as long-term contracts, would not be subject to it. And Ronald Reagan certainly would not use his line-item veto on the defense budget.

REPRESENTATIVE CHENEY: I do not argue that the line-item veto is the cure for all the problems. But the president would have some additional authority to impose more discipline on the process. I do not think that is wrong. I think it is sound.

Norm's argument that the line-item veto is somehow a radical departure does not hold water in light of the fact that forty-three out of fifty governors already have that authority.

MR. DALY: But it really goes beyond that, doesn't it? We had a long history, from the 1880s to now, of very strong support for the line-item veto, from Grant, Hays, Arthur, F.D.R., Truman, and Eisenhower. And the Congress itself gave the governors of our territories a line-item veto that they denied to the White House.

DR. ORNSTEIN: I am not surprised to find that presidents have wanted a line-item veto authority. Throughout history, I would be surprised if we found one who did not. And I am not surprised that Dick Cheney thinks a line-item veto is a good idea. He spent time in the White House, and he has a presidential perspective. [Laughter] I imagine Jim thinks it is a good idea too. But I believe a line-item veto will not discipline spending. No evidence from the states suggests it does.

Indeed, I believe that presidents have more of a bias for spending than Congress. They are in office for a short period of time, and they want to get things done. No president is immune to that.

Though the line-item veto would apply to a small portion of the budget, it is a portion that matters a great deal to members of Congress, even if to a diminishing degree. The veto would give the president almost a blackmail authority to accomplish other goals with the Congress.

If Ronald Reagan had the line-item veto authority, he would

77

not use it, in the end, to cut spending. For instance, he wanted more MX missiles than Congress gave him. If he had had the line-item veto, he would have said to members of Congress, "You want to clean up the Chesapeake Bay? You want that dam or bridge? I'll axe it through the line-item veto unless you vote for more MX missiles." We would get more bridges, more dams, more cleanups, more MX missiles, and more spending.

REPRESENTATIVE PANETTA: The part not mentioned very often is that he does have that power now. He can exercise a veto on a bill. The argument is, "Well, gee, there are some areas where he supports legislation." Baloney. If presidents want to exercise a veto on a spending bill, they ought to exercise it.

This president has been hesitant to exercise the veto on spending bills. Furthermore, presidents have the power to send a rescission back to the Congress. If the president wants to rescind funding in a particular area, he can send that rescission to the Congress, and the Congress then has the power to reject or accept it. He has the power to initiate that now and, frankly, the Congress goes along with most of those rescissions. So the president does have the power to exercise a degree of control over spending under the present system.

DR. MILLER: The president can send a rescission message, but unless the houses of Congress act within forty-five days it is dead. A substantial rescission message therefore will not be acted upon unless the majority of Congress believes that certain spending is not opportune. Usually this happens right after Congress has, in fact, appropriated those accounts. But let me go back to what has happened in the budget process this time.

Despite having a budget resolution that directs the Appropriations committees to meet certain targets, those committees this fall have continually come up with spending amounts that exceed the limits specified in the Congressional Budget Resolution. In one case, the president vetoed the Treasury/Postal appropriations. So the president is not reluctant to use the veto pen where the appropriations get out of hand, and he will do so.

REPRESENTATIVE PANETTA: Jim, as you know, there is a numbers game that goes on between the White House and the Hill. Scoring is a problem. We use the Congressional Budget Office to score, and it has been the viewpoint of the Budget Committee that those bills fit within our targets. Your viewpoint is that they do not. That creates a lot of conflict in itself. One useful step would be for everybody to agree on the basic numbers. We do not even have that at the present time.

DR. MILLER: That is a good suggestion because there *are* differences over scoring—for instance, whether appropriations passed a year before and then held in abeyance should count this year or not. But games are played, arguably on the executive as well as the congressional side. For example, there was an overcharge in the Blue Cross/Blue Shield insurance policy, so they are going to give some kind of refund. They will refund part of the money to government employees and part to the government itself. But in the reconciliation stage, they counted not only the money returned to the government, but the money being returned to the employees as savings. Of course, that's phony.

REPRESENTATIVE PANETTA: Well, nobody argues that games are not played. [Laughter]
Let me tell you, that's true on both sides.

DR. ORNSTEIN: I'd like to get back to Dick Cheney's question: If a constitutional solution won't work, what should we do? A constitutional solution is not the answer. I'd like to see many structural changes. One of the salutary things about the Gramm-Rudman notion is that it emphasizes developing a concurrence on assumptions between the executive branch and the Congress, taking it out of the realm of politics, where it's been for many, many years and where it should not be. Structural changes can provide differences at the margins.

For instance, I think the idea of a summit differs from the notion of all the leaders simply getting together in a room in one important way. As I suggested earlier, a fundamental part of our problem is that even though the public sees the deficit as the number one issue, it is not a lapel-grabber for people out in the country. I would wager, Dick, that when you go back home to Wyoming, you don't have a lot of people coming up to you and saying, "Do something about the deficit and do it now."

People are relatively content. To solve this problem, we have to send a message to the public that the elites regard this as a terrifying problem, one that has to be dealt with now.

A summit raises awareness to a higher level, I think, and would create a greater consensus. It might also create a greater consensus among elites. Right now there's no consensus with the president, the House or the Senate that the deficit is the biggest problem in the country.

Having done that we might create a protective umbrella for the top leadership, where some would be willing to give a little on revenues, others a little on social security and other entitlement programs, and so on. Finally we would get to the big-ticket items, where we really have to make some changes.

REPRESENTATIVE CHENEY: Norm, if you travel with me back to my district, you'd see there are people waiting for me when I get off the airplane who grab me by the lapels. That's why I'm a politician and you're a political scientist. [Laughter]

I think the concern is definitely there, in the nation. We have to spend more time on the problem. A lot needs to be done with public education. But I'm not prepared to say that all we need is a political consensus or a negotiated arrangement or leadership and congressional cooperation to solve the problem.

The process doesn't work now. We're spending an enormous amount of time on it—a subject we haven't even talked about. I think Leon Panetta would agree with me, one thing that's appalling about the process is that we spend all of our time on the budget, and so we don't get anything else done.

REPRESENTATIVE PANETTA: That's right.

REPRESENTATIVE CHENEY: Why not consider a biennial budget process? Let's go to a two-year instead of a twelve-month cycle. The Constitution would allow a two-year cycle.

We could save a lot of time, so that we would have better oversight on the programs. Maybe we'd find it far more efficient and less painful to do this once every twenty-four months, instead of once every twelve months.

There are procedural changes we can look at—some constitutional, some statutory—and we shouldn't reject them out of hand, by arguing that all we need is a political consensus to solve the problem.

REPRESENTATIVE PANETTA: I agree that steps can be taken to improve the present process. I happen to agree with the two-year budget approach, and have introduced legislation proposing a two-year budget process.

In addition to that, enforcement tools need to be improved. Nonetheless, no matter what kind of time frame we set, we have to have the leadership to meet those time frames. For example, we're not completing our appropriations bills now because everybody knows how to play the game of a continuing resolution at the end of the year.

Instead of passing thirteen separate appropriations bills the way we should, the game now is to hold back and not pass them all, because we can wrap them up in one big train, the continuing resolution.

Then we can bury within that train all the various pieces we want, and they won't be subject to individual amendments. It's horrendous.

REPRESENTATIVE CHENEY: And they won't be subject to presidential veto. That's a classic way that the Congress thwarts the president's existing authority to veto. But if he had a line-item veto, he'd be able to discourage the whole continuing resolution process.

MR. DALY: Let's get down to particulars. Representative Panetta, you have introduced an amendment to create a biennial budget cycle. Why do you think that could be particularly beneficial? After all, congressmen are elected for two years. Wouldn't this, to some degree, compromise their abilities to participate?

REPRESENTATIVE PANETTA: I first introduced this amendment ten years ago when I joined the Budget Committee because even then I thought we were spending too much time operating on a crisis basis in dealing with the budget. We'd no sooner complete one budget cycle than we were fighting the battle over the next budget cycle. A set of constituents would ask, "What's happening on education funding?" and next thing you know, they'd come in and ask, "What's happening on the next set?" Then we'd have a set of supplementals in between, so it was constant.

I view the whole Gramm-Rudman approach as turning up the heat on the budget process about 300 degrees. We will be spending a lot more time dealing with nothing else but budget issues. Rather than fighting the budget resolution battle every year, we ought to spend a year in our process doing oversight, evaluating programs—

REPRESENTATIVE CHENEY: Yes.

REPRESENTATIVE PANETTA: —seeing how effective they are, and whether they're working or not. Then we could spend the next year appropriating or targeting the funding for those areas. This, first of all, allows more time for planning.

Second, we can begin to focus a lot more on oversight of existing programs, rather than simply operating on a day-to-day basis, trying to save whatever programs are out there whether they're working or not.

And, third, it would establish a little more stability over a longer time frame and replace the chaotic process we have in place now.

The objection has been that a two-year Congress wants to be able to deal with the budget every year, because that's how members of some of these committees exercise their power. The Appropriations Committee is number one in this respect.

We have made some progress; the proposals from the so-called Beilenson Task Force called for at least two-year authorizations. I'm hoping we can extend that to appropriations, as well.

Dr. Ornstein: I don't disagree with the notion of a two-year budget cycle, although I doubt very much it would have the intended effect. Right now, we have a budget process where we set economic assumptions for a time twenty-one months in advance, and we spend a lot of the time during the budget cycle tinkering with those assumptions because they have a big effect on what goes into the budget.

We know we aren't perfect even if we make the best, most honest effort forecasting. I can just imagine what would happen if we had to set our assumptions thirty-four months in advance.

But I'll agree that this would be a good step forward. There are many other steps that would also be good, but they are at the margins, they're incremental.

It would be wonderful if we could reduce the $200 billion deficit to $185 billion by working out these little details on appropriations bills—and a billion here, a billion there does add up. And it would be nice if we could do more things than just the budget, if we weren't so preoccupied with it.

But they don't get to the gut issues. What worries me about the proposed constitutional changes is, to a degree, the American people have been sold a bill of goods. It is a foolish notion that, if we just make a constitutional change, or tinker with the structures, then we'll solve this problem without pain—as if all we have to do is get a constitutional amendment to balance the budget. Right now the problem is the people who don't have the guts to make the painful decisions say we only need to eliminate the waste, fraud, and abuse, or the programs that only benefit the special interests (and none of us are special interests, of course—we are not beneficiaries of those programs).

The basic problem is not to balance the budget, it is to get down to a tolerable deficit, which my AEI colleague John Makin and I would say is about 2 percent of the gross national product instead of the present 5 percent, and that will require painful things that will hurt a lot of people.

It will hurt farmers and all the nonfarmers in rural areas who benefit from those programs. They don't consider themselves to be special interests. It will hurt social security recipients. It will hurt those who want a bigger defense budget.

We cannot let people believe that there's a simple answer to this problem—that if we just adjust the structures, in a big way or a little way, it will solve the problem. It's going to take pain.

REPRESENTATIVE CHENEY: Norm, I don't disagree with anything you've said. Of course it's going to take pain. Of course decisions are going to be difficult.

But we're trying to find ways to bias the process more in the direction of those kinds of decisions, to reach the consensus we aren't reaching at present. We are willing to tamper with the process in order to do that.

The argument that there's no change that can strengthen the president's hand or the congressional hand and thereby make us better budgeteers, doesn't hold water. To urge that a line-item veto constitutional amendment wouldn't help the budget process, when we use it today in forty-three states, or that the biennial process wouldn't help, when we use it in a number of states as well, or that constitutional provisions specifying the relationship between outlays and income wouldn't have some benefit, flies in the face of 200 years of experience at the state level.

We have a federal system. We have tried a lot of these concepts at the state level. Obviously, the federal government is different, but it has a lot of similarities, too, and we ought to take advantage of state experience and expertise, and see if there aren't in fact ways that we can improve the process, improve the procedures, improve the Constitution.

DR. MILLER: The Act of 1974, arguably, transferred some authority from the president, who had some rescission authority, to the Congress. The line-item veto would transfer some power, some authority, from the Congress to the president.

One of the major drafters of the Gramm-Rudman-Hollings proposal, Phil Gramm, said that one of his objectives was to be neutral with respect to the transfer of authority so it would put both the president and the Congress on the same plane. He thought this was a key to enacting legislation changing the institutional arrangements, so that the budget deficit would be dealt with.

We have two outstanding members of Congress here. I wonder how they feel about the transfer of power. I guess Dick Cheney is saying that he does not object to transferring some power from the Congress to the president. Do your colleagues agree with you on that?

REPRESENTATIVE CHENEY: I would see the line-item veto as a restitution of the balance between branches that existed for 100 years and that was changed by the 1974 act when we wiped out the impound-ment authority of the president.

As John Charles Daly pointed out in his opening remarks, presi-dents from Grant in the 1860s to Nixon in the 1970s were able to impound funds. Some of the proposals that have been discussed would simply restore what I believe to be the appropriate balance and give the president some additional authority.

REPRESENTATIVE PANETTA: I dare say that some people who support a line-item veto assume that Ronald Reagan will be president forever—

REPRESENTATIVE CHENEY: That's another constitutional amendment we could work on [Laughter]

REPRESENTATIVE PANETTA: —and don't recognize that a Teddy Ken-nedy or someone like that might exercise the same kind of power. I just want to get back to the bottom line: No matter how we change the process or the procedure, it still depends a great deal on the willing-ness of people in office to exercise leadership on these issues.

The whole thrust behind Gramm-Rudman is that it's a club. My God, here we are in a democratic society saying that we have to fashion a club to force people to do what they should be doing.

The Senate argues that the reason for Gramm-Rudman is to force the president to come up with the revenue if he wants a larger defense budget. Others argue that Gramm-Rudman will force us to do something about entitlement programs.

It's a sad commentary when we have to resort to clubs to force us to do what we should be doing anyway.

DR. MILLER: Can I tell you what I think is a sad commentary? I think we would all agree that trying to eliminate the deficit tomorrow would be a mistake. So Gramm-Rudman calls for it to decrease over a period of years. It requires the president to propose a budget at a target level, and it requires Congress to pass a budget with no greater than that level of deficit. If they don't agree on a budget, then there is se-questering, or across-the-board cuts in spending, with social security exempted.

The drafters of the bill and certainly the president view the se-questering process as the absolute last resort. That's something that we don't want to happen. It would take place only if the process failed.

But I find it perplexing and amusing that by far the most debate over Gramm-Rudman-Hollings focused on the sequestering process.

I once characterized it this way. I said to one of my teen-age children one Saturday morning, "Tonight, if you don't come in by curfew, you can't watch your favorite TV program on Sunday." And instead of figuring how to get in by curfew, he spent all the rest of the day arguing with me about the nature of the punishment on Sunday.

Why doesn't Congress have enough self-confidence to believe the process would work? It's the same process that is incorporated in the 1974 Budget Act, with just the addition of meeting a deficit target.

REPRESENTATIVE PANETTA: I think you've raised a very important issue. Gramm-Rudman is not only a club, it's also an escape for members of Congress. Why should members of Congress vote responsibly for cuts in appropriations bills in the reconciliation process, when they can simply let this thing hit the trigger, and cuts would occur across the board? The process would somehow take the blame.

That is the danger in Gramm-Rudman. A lot of members will say, "Why should I vote for a tough budget that will cut social security, that will cut defense, that will raise taxes, when I can simply vote the kind of budget I prefer, and have no budget adopted? Then we can go right to this trigger."

The danger is that it undermines the budget process. It creates a club, but it doesn't create a carrot to do the right thing.

MR. DALY: May I have the first question, please?

MARK CANNON, staff director for the Constitution Bicentennial Commission: If I understand Professor Ornstein, he suggested there was no congressional bias toward deficits, because throughout much of our history we had either run surpluses or only minor deficits. I can think of three major changes, though, between the first century-and-a-half of our history and the last half-century that bear on this.

One, we had a vast amount of land earlier that we sold, and so raised revenues with minimal pain. Two, we had tariffs that supplied substantial revenues with minimal pain, at least as perceived by the people. Three, until Beardsley Ruml, we never had the painless system of paying taxes, where it's taken out automatically.

These are three major factors that may have given Congress an institutional bias against deficits in the earlier period.

Isn't the problem here the transcendent problem of a constitutional democracy, a tendency to sacrifice long-term gain for short-term gain?

DR. ORNSTEIN: Clearly, there have been some important changes, although it is not entirely true that we could balance the budget in the eighteenth and nineteenth centuries because we had painless sources of revenue from selling land or from tariffs.

If you look at some of the congressional debates over the budget during that time, you see that they incurred substantial pain, particularly since they tried not only to balance the budget, but also to run surpluses, first to overcome the debt from the Revolutionary War, then the debt from the War of 1812, and so on.

It was painful. It was difficult. But they overcame the difficulties.

In fact, with the exception of the two world wars, we continued into the 1960s to alleviate a substantial portion of the debt from the wars by running surpluses during peace.

I just don't think that the American political or constitutional system creates a fundamental bias toward out-of-control deficits. We have not run out of control through most of our history, and the changes of the past twenty years, including the reforms in Congress, would not themselves have led to the enormous deficits that we have run, particularly in the last five years.

As to the second part of your question, about constitutional democracies being unwilling to take short-term pain for a long-term gain, that is a flaw in human nature, I suspect. There aren't many people anywhere who are willing to take short-term pain for the uncertain prospect of long-term gain. That clearly is a problem. We have a public that by and large says, "Hey, what we're doing is the equivalent of a perpetual sale. We're getting a dollar's worth of services at a 20 percent discount. We're only paying 80 cents for it."

It's the responsibility of elites to overcome that attitude, and to persuade people to incur that short-term pain. Instead, the political elites have lulled the people into a false sense of security.

The 1984 election campaign suggested to people that there's no reason to take short-term pain because we're doing wonderfully. But that's not a flaw in the basic system. It's something we can overcome, as we have overcome it through most of our history.

REPRESENTATIVE CHENEY: I'm inclined to agree with Mr. Cannon, that things are different today. I buy Norm Ornstein's argument that the original notion of indexing social security was in response to the 20 percent increases in social security benefits Congress approved in election years.

But Congress has put on the books a whole bunch of programs that simply weren't there in 1960—often in response to presidential initiative or support. In 1960, we didn't have a Medicaid or Medicare program. Social security spending was still relatively modest in those days, because we didn't have as many people drawing benefits. We didn't have a food stamp program. We didn't have aid to elementary and secondary education.

All those programs were put on the books in the 1960s followed by enormous increases in funding in the 1960s and the 1970s. We have to understand that the emphasis in Congress over the years has been heavily toward more funding for domestic programs. This simply didn't exist before we started running big government.

REPRESENTATIVE PANETTA: I would say there is an institutional bias against tough decisions in basically three areas—the three areas that must be addressed in the context of the deficits that we're facing. For whatever reason, nobody is willing to take that first step.

Decisions here will involve sacrifices that will affect a lot of voters. All this will make it harder for Congress and the president to do what needs to be done.

Our system operates in either of two ways. The president and the Congress can lead, although I'm not sure that 535 members can really exercise much leadership. We basically represent our own districts and operate fairly independently.

Or, without that leadership working together to try to find answers, the system operates on the basis of crisis. The reality is that the deficit is still not at the crisis point.

Yes, we see it in the trade balance. Yes, people are beginning to be concerned about facing it down the road, but it still hasn't hit. To a large extent that is undermining the efforts to solve the problem.

REPRESENTATIVE CHENEY: But, Leon, you can't get away with the argument that there was not an enormous increase in spending by Congress in the past twenty years, when we went from a $100-billion to a trillion-dollar budget, a 900 percent increase.

REPRESENTATIVE PANETTA: Nobody disagrees with that, Dick. As I said, there's enough blame to go around; but, right now, the nature of the budget demands action in three areas.

REPRESENTATIVE CHENEY: That's a convenient argument, but entitlements encompass a great many of these programs I mentioned. So the institutional bias, for the past twenty years, has been in that direction.

DR. ORNSTEIN: But why did those programs come about? Was there suddenly some dramatic change in the institutions that caused them to run hog wild in the 1960s? Most of the programs you talked about, Dick, came about in a very short period. They were the Great Society programs, pushed through by the president—that office you want to give great additional authority.

REPRESENTATIVE CHENEY: But that was Lyndon Johnson, with a two-to-one Democratic majority in both houses of Congress.

DR. ORNSTEIN: Well, there'll be another Lyndon Johnson down the road. It was chiefly the president pushing those programs through.

REPRESENTATIVE CHENEY: But Congress, clearly, has played a major role in the massive increase in spending over the past twenty years. The institutional bias is there today.

DR. ORNSTEIN: But some of those programs—many of them, in fact—have been restrained pretty dramatically in the past few years.

REPRESENTATIVE CHENEY: Not enough.

DR. ORNSTEIN: Perhaps not enough, but it's the big items that we haven't gotten to. If we had made some of these constitutional changes giving more authority to the president before this era, our problem would be far worse. Lyndon Johnson would have gotten even more than he got, with that additional authority.

DR. MILLER: I think that we're beginning to agree—and I even hear Norm saying it—that we have an institutional imperfection. The question is how to address it. It's not just the wrong people in office. I think we have good people in Congress—

REPRESENTATIVE CHENEY: Even if they are for pork. [Laughter]

DR. MILLER: —and we have a good president.

REPRESENTATIVE CHENEY: We have a splendid president. [Laughter]

DR. MILLER: But the point is that we have an institutional bias that yields deficits, and we need to address that institutional bias through something like a Gramm-Rudman social compact or through a constitutional amendment for a balanced budget.

REPRESENTATIVE PANETTA: For once, let's slice through the academic baloney. [Laughter]
We have to control the growth in defense; we have to control the

growth in entitlements; and we have to raise revenues. Now, that's the bottom line.

We can talk about academics, we can talk about institutional bias, but that's the bottom line. So the question is: Why aren't we doing something on this issue?

MR. DALY: Why haven't I heard "cut entitlements"; "cut defense"?

REPRESENTATIVE PANETTA: That's the way we talk to our constituents. We say, "Limit the growth." [Laughter] That's another way to say "cut."

MR. DALY: I think we need another question.

PROFESSOR HERMAN BELZ, University of Maryland: One issue that's unclear from this discussion is how alarmed public opinion is about the deficits. A second issue that hasn't been discussed is that the federal government has taken the place of the states as the primary regulator of everyday life, in employment, welfare, education and so forth. As the federal government does that, surely there will be a need for constitutional adjustment, so the federal government can handle the budgetary process the way the states have handled it. Governors have had the line-item veto. States have had longer, more detailed, constitutions, into which people put things that we, at the national level, regard as legislative. But with the shift in responsibilities, more things will have to be dealt with in the U.S. Constitution as well.

My question is: If public concern is growing, as I think it is, and if that is expressed in the call for a second constitutional convention or a constitutional amendment, then what is wrong with the people, as the constituent power, changing the constitutional system to make the adjustment referred to? I sense apprehension about this on the part of many of you.

REPRESENTATIVE PANETTA: No one disagrees that the public can do whatever it wants on the issue. Nobody will stop the public from proceeding if, in fact, it wants a constitutional amendment.

But I don't think the public ought to be under the false assumption that passing a balanced-budget amendment will solve the problem of the deficit, or of the balance between the federal and state governments. That just is not the case. I see a few hundred ways to get around any balanced-budget amendment approach.

For instance, you can take programs off budget. The result is that deficits would continue to go up, and we would continue to play the same games. I just don't want people to believe that there is somehow a magic answer.

MR. DALY: Would you define "off-budget" and describe its impact on the total economic picture?

REPRESENTATIVE PANETTA: Sure. We provide direct spending for on-budget items. Entitlement programs are on-budget items. But other areas have been designated off-budget by Congress, such as the Strategic Petroleum Reserve. There's now an effort to put social security off-budget, which means that it would not be reflected in the basic budget or, for that matter, in the deficit. There is also a credit budget, which is regarded as off-budget. Moving areas from on-budget to off-budget seems to reduce the problem, but doesn't really reduce it because we are still spending in those particular areas.

DR. ORNSTEIN: I won't spend much time on the broader question of whether we ought to rewrite our Constitution dramatically to bring in more detail, because I don't think many people would want to do that. But let me talk about the states and the notion that we ought to adopt nationally provisions that the states have, because of the way that they've operated in the past. If we do that, maybe we ought to give authority for national defense to governors. Obviously, we don't want to do that, because we realize that our system at the national level is a very different one.

What lessons can we learn from the states? Most information about line-item vetoes—and we're now getting significant detail on how they have worked in the states—suggests that they have not resulted in significant savings. Let me add that most states that brag about their constitutional provisions to balance the budget—and that have governors who go around the country boasting that they have made the tough decisions—eliminate capital expenditures from their budgets.

The budgets include only operating expenditures, not expenditures for longer-term capital reasons. The federal government doesn't do that.

If it did what the states did—if it took out what the Office of Management and Budget defines in the budget as capital expenditures—we wouldn't have a problem. We could say we were close to balancing the budget, and we could come to an agreement on how we would balance what was left. But the problem would still remain.

So states do not balance their budgets. They take items like highways and buildings and automobiles off the budget, and finance them through bonds which, of course, means incurring debt.

The analogy between the federal government and the states isn't appropriate. We have no evidence that what has worked in the states would work in the federal government.

REPRESENTATIVE CHENEY: I don't think that all wisdom resides in Washington. We have fifty states out there, with a wealth of experience that we ought to be willing to look at. The bright, able people who serve as governors and state legislators have had some lessons that they might be willing to share with us. To suggest that, somehow, provisions that have been in force at the state level—in some cases for 200 years—cannot be applied at the federal level, seems to me ludicrous on its face.

DR. MILLER: We can learn a lot from the states and how they go about their budget process. Norm is right that some states find it easier to meet their constitutional balanced-budget requirements by using capital budgets, but I still think we can learn a lot.

ROBERT A. GOLDWIN, American Enterprise Institute: Where the power of the purse is placed in any regime is a good indication of how that society is constituted. For instance, there was a great fear here of letting the executive have access to the purse, because that was always the signpost of tyranny. Any executive who could get public money without having it appropriated by law had all the earmarks of a tyrant.

The whole idea of giving the power of the purse to Congress is that those most directly elected by the people are thought to be the most accountable in spending public money. But our experience seems to be—whether it's an institutional bias or a temporary situation or whatever—that Congress doesn't do a very good job of exercising the power of the purse. And although the executive branch may have more budgetary expertise, we don't trust them with it.

The question, then, is: Is there some way to combine trustworthiness and capability—whether it's by unusual leadership or a new spirit of cooperation or some new devices—so that those who appropriate and those who spend public money can be trusted and capable?

REPRESENTATIVE CHENEY: As Mr. Panetta said earlier—and as Barber Conable, the distinguished former member of the House, has also said over the years—the system does respond in a crisis and, often, difficult decisions are not made until there is a crisis. If the Founding Fathers had wanted an efficient mechanism, obviously they would have created a very different system from the one they did create.

Public concern will be great enough in the next few years to come to grips with the deficit. A national consensus will have to be developed, and we'll do it through new procedures or summit meetings or major compromises.

There is no automatic fix for the system. There are marginal fixes that would make it easier. Changing the process would help, and constitutional amendments or modifications would help. But in the end, as others have suggested tonight, it will take national concern that this is more important than any other problem we face. Then we will come to grips with the issue, just as we did a few years ago with social security.

When we reached the point where the social security system was about to go belly-up, then the administration and Congress came together, and worked out a solution.

DR. MILLER: In the context of government organization, I think our Founding Fathers did provide us with a very efficient decision-making process. It's a process that translates the demands of ordinary citizens into government goods and services. In this respect, tyrants would be very inefficient. They might make decisions quickly, but those decisions wouldn't mesh with the desires of the people.

On the question of expertise, one major advantage of the 1974 act was the establishment of the Congressional Budget Office, headed now by Rudy Penner, former fellow at the American Enterprise Institute. That has provided enormous expertise to the budget committees and to other members of Congress for their oversight of activities.

MR. DALY: Have enough information resources been created so that the Congress has what it needs, the administration has what it needs, and the public has what it needs to make reasonable and responsible decisions with respect to the economy and the budget?

REPRESENTATIVE PANETTA: The information sources are there, in both the Congressional Budget Office on the Hill and the administration's Office of Management and Budget. We struggle sometimes, but we can always track a particular line item or number. But as we mentioned earlier, there is a lack of consensus on how to treat certain budget items—as an entitlement, for example, or as discretionary spending. That can be significant in trying to reduce the budget. It would be in the public interest for OMB and CBO to come together on their assumptions, so that we have a common base for projecting into the future. The information is there, but sometimes it conflicts, and that hurts.

DR. ORNSTEIN: If there's a problem of information, it's a problem with a misinformed public. If you asked what is in the budget, the public probably would say that $600 toilet seats and $7,000 coffee makers make up a third of the defense budget and a sixth of the budget overall; that waste, fraud, abuse, and welfare programs make up at least half of what remains of the budget, and that essential services are what's left.

The real make-up of the budget, the 85 percent figure that Leon mentioned, is not something that most Americans are aware of. If they were, they'd have a different perspective on this issue.

JOHN MAKIN, American Enterprise Institute: We're talking about the deficit as if it is an awful thing, bad enough to require a change in the Constitution. And, yet, Congress and the president make projections about the deficit based on the assumption that the economy will continue to grow at a rate of 3, 4, 5 percent, or whatever. In other words, things are going to continue to be fine.

Let me ask Jim Miller: How can we persuade the public to bear all the pain involved in dealing with the deficit while we're saying the economy is in great shape and looks even better next year?

DR. MILLER: I don't have an easy answer to that. There will be some pain in eliminating or reducing the deficit over time.

In an ideal world we would have a deficit that was not constant over time. We might run a surplus some times, a deficit other times. But the experience we've had indicates a substantial institutional bias toward deficit finance, for the reasons we've talked about. Only a constitutional amendment or a Gramm-Rudman approach will address that bias.

At times we might still want to run a surplus or a deficit, but those imperfections pale in comparison with the ones we are experiencing today.

REPRESENTATIVE PANETTA: Mr. Makin has raised a good point. Where we want to go within a period is somewhat arbitrary, because all of our numbers depend on a set of assumptions about where the economy is going, what the unemployment rate will be, what the inflation rate will be and what the interest rates are likely to be.

These assumptions are all based on projections of what will happen in the next fiscal year. Nobody really knows that, although the projections can be fairly close.

Administrations will generally project positive results in the next year. They are not going to project a recession. They are optimistic in their projections, so we have a battle over the basic assumptions. Even if we had a consensus on those assumptions, the next year we could have some dramatic changes just by virtue of what happens within the economy.

All these things need to be considered whenever an arbitary target is set. One concern I have about Gramm-Rudman is that when we say we will reach a certain point by a certain date, we fail to consider what may happen in the economy. If we run into a serious recession, do we want to cut spending to the extent that Gramm-Rudman demands and force an even deeper recession as a result?

Those areas of concern haven't been addressed in the process changes now taking place on the Hill.

Mr. Daly: Next question, please?

Phil Lyons, U.S. Civil Rights Commission: My question has to do with the resources that may be found within the original Constitution for dealing with the problem of skyrocketing budget deficits. *The Federalist* papers talk about the problem of interest groups having an undue influence in the legislature. That leads to the observation that today's monopolization of programs and responsibilities by the federal government is precisely the opposite of what the framers intended. Why not look to the original Constitution and argue for a devolution of program responsibilities back to the states? That would certainly lessen the problem in the federal government.

Dr. Ornstein: The Constitution and discussion that surrounded it in *The Federalist* papers anticipated plenty and are perfectly adequate to deal with the problem.

If James Madison were here today and got over some of the shocks from what he saw, he would argue that we are, in fact, dealing with the mischief of factions better than ever in the past and in precisely the way he suggested—with a multiplication of factions that work against each other, thus providing substantial leeway for the institutions to operate.

As for a devolution to the states, I don't object. We're seeing a substantial devolution of some power and authority to the states. Unfortunately, I suspect, as resources dwindle, the federal government, under Democrats and Republicans alike, will step in and put even more constraints on what the states can do. That's a serious problem.

We will have to address that a few years down the road; but I don't think that a constitutional change would make things any better right now.

REPRESENTATIVE CHENEY: The Reagan administration has, in fact, tried the approach suggested.

We have moved toward block grants, for example, trying to free up state responsibilities and requirements as we've reduced funding levels. I think it has basically been sound. Unfortunately, it has often been thwarted by the Congress, responding to the special interest groups that can't get the funding at the state level and argue for it from Washington. So it is a good suggestion, but I think unfortunately, it doesn't fit with the political situation we face today.

REPRESENTATIVE PANETTA: But one person's special interest group is another person's constituency. Every constituency is part of some kind of special interest, whether it's senior citizens or some minority group or the banking community or the agricultural community. Those are special interests, and to some extent, all of them represent our constituents. They have a right to try to influence what happens here, and that will not change by returning powers to the state.

KATE STIFF, Yale Law School: In the initial description of the fiscal powers in the Constitution no mention was made of the appropriations clause, which requires that no money be drawn from the Treasury except in consequence of an appropriation by law. "By law"— that's by the Congress and the president acting in their legislative capacities. Might one suggest that the move toward greater off-budget funding and entitlement programs, with either trust funds or permanent appropriations, is not in keeping with at least the spirit of the appropriations clause?

That clause is often looked at, as was mentioned earlier, as a means of keeping the sovereign from spending money without Congress approving. But it is also, it seems to me, a requirement that the president and the Congress, in their legislative capacities, stand up and be counted. Isn't the current implementation of the appropriations clause partly a reason for the increase in expenditures without full political control?

REPRESENTATIVE PANETTA: I don't disagree with your concern about that trend. The institutions have tried to insulate certain areas from year-to-year budget attacks.

To maintain infrastructure, for instance, the proceeds from a tax on gasoline are put into a trust fund for highways, the effort there is so that they will not be attacked day by day.

The same is true for entitlements. We create an entitlement so that we don't have to fight from year to year over who will qualify for food stamps, and so forth.

95

As another example, concern over attacks on social security lead people to try to insulate it by taking it off-budget. That takes away more and more of our accountability to the public. That's at the heart of the problem we're dealing with here. Ultimately, we have to be held accountable to the public. The public has to say whether we did or we didn't do our job as the Constitution intended. And when we play these games of moving things off-budget, or when we look to procedural ways to solve a problem, we avoid the accountability that is the heart and soul of our democratic system.

MR. DALY: This concludes another public policy forum presented by the American Enterprise Institute for Public Policy Research.

4

Affirmative Action and the Constitution

William B. Allen
John Charles Daly
Drew S. Days III
Benjamin L. Hooks
William Bradford Reynolds

J OHN CHARLES DALY, former ABC News chief: This public policy forum, one of a series presented by the American Enterprise Institute, will examine the conflicts involved in the task of combating all kinds of discrimination and striving for equality of Americans under the Constitution. Our subject: affirmative action and the Constitution.

Few issues of the day so divide our nation as current affirmative action policies, especially when numerical goals are used to increase minority group opportunities in employment or admissions to college and professional schools. One side contends that such policies are necessary to ensure an equality of results, to be sure of achieving equality of opportunity. The other side argues that such preferences are unconstitutional reverse discrimination.

Can we achieve equality of opportunity in America without race-, sex-, or ethnic-conscious remedies for discrimination? Is it just and constitutional to deny a qualified person an equal chance for a job by giving someone else a preference, to redress past injustices or to eliminate present discrimination? Are there group rights under the Constitution of the United States, or does the Constitution require that individual rights predominate in every instance?

To help us find answers to these questions, we have a very distinguished panel. On my far right is Dr. William B. Allen, professor of government in the Department of Humanities and Social Sciences at Harvey Mudd College in California. Dr. Allen is a member of the National Council on the Humanities and of the California State Advisory Committee of the U.S. Commission on Civil Rights.

On my immediate right is the Honorable Wm. Bradford Reynolds, who has been assistant attorney general in charge of the Civil Rights Division since 1981. Previously he was a partner in the law firm of Shaw, Pittman, Potts, and Trowbridge and was an assistant to the solicitor general of the United States.

On my immediate left is Dr. Benjamin L. Hooks, who has been executive director of the National Association for the Advancement of Colored People (NAACP) since 1977. Dr. Hooks is chairman of the Leadership Conference on Civil Rights and is the past chairman of the Black Leadership Forum. He is also an ordained minister on leave from the Middle Baptist Church in Memphis, Tennessee.

On my far left is the Honorable Drew S. Days III, associate professor of law at Yale Law School. From 1977 to 1980, during the Carter administration, Professor Days was assistant attorney general in charge of the Civil Rights Division. Previously, he was the first assistant counsel to the NAACP Legal Defense and Educational Fund.

The history of discrimination in our country is a long and familiar one. Our Constitution was written almost two centuries ago, at a time when black slavery was an entrenched institution. The tensions between the principles undergirding our nation and the fact of slavery led us to a Civil War out of which emerged three amendments to the Constitution, the so-called Reconstruction amendments.

The Thirteenth Amendment abolished slavery, and the Fifteenth secured the right to vote, but it is the Fourteenth Amendment that is chiefly relied on to define equality and civil rights in America. That amendment reads in part, "No state shall deprive any person of life, liberty or property without due process of law, nor deny to any person within its jurisdiction the equal protection of the laws."

It was not until 1954, however, that the Supreme Court in *Brown* v. *Board of Education* ended legal segregation of public school children by race. There ensued through the 1960s a long train of legislation to secure civil rights in America.

Today, new policies requiring the hiring and promotion of blacks, women, and other minorities have been adopted to eliminate what is often called invidious discrimination. The debate over affirmative action programs continues, and the Supreme Court in a string of cases has been less than clear in its efforts to pronounce on which forms of affirmative action policies are constitutional and which are not.

To come to grips with the questions and issues that we face tonight, gentlemen, let me ask the same question of each of you: Do affirmative action policies that involve racial, sex, or ethnic classifications conform to the letter and the spirit of the Constitution?

WM. BRADFORD REYNOLDS, assistant attorney general: If we review the debates in the Thirty-ninth and the succeeding Congress and the debates surrounding ratification of the Fourteenth Amendment, it is clear beyond doubt that the intent of the amendment was to command that all government decisions be made on a race-neutral basis; that the amendment was meant to guarantee equal opportunity, not equal results; and that it would not permit preferences by reason of race. Any kind of action, whether a quota, goal, or any other affirmative action measure, granting preference by reason of race is contrary to both the letter and the spirit of that constitutional amendment.

BENJAMIN L. HOOKS, executive director, NAACP: I think that is absolutely wrong. Article I, section 2, clause 3, of the Constitution itself starts off with a quota: 3/5. That is how black folks were counted in that original Constitution.

There is no question in the mind of any competent scholar that the Thirteenth, Fourteenth, and Fifteenth amendments were written for one purpose: to eliminate the practice of slavery and the possible perpetuation of segregation. The Thirteenth Amendment abolished slavery. White folks did not need that. The Fifteenth Amendment guaranteed the right to vote regardless of color; white people did not need that. The Fourteenth Amendment provided for equal protection under the law, and that amendment would not have existed were the purpose not to abolish slavery.

The Nineteenth Amendment guaranteed women the right to vote. So the Constitution itself has recognized that there is color in this world, that there are sexes in this world, and that from time to time we must use those categories to achieve the Constitution's goals. The Thirteenth, Fourteenth, and Fifteenth amendments—the Reconstruction amendments—were written specifically to deal with questions of color. To interpret them otherwise seems to me vain and foolhardy.

WILLIAM B. ALLEN, professor of government, Harvey Mudd College: It is misleading to call affirmative action reverse discrimination, as we often do. There is no such thing, any more than the opposite of injustice, for example, is reverse injustice. Affirmative action is discrimination pure and simple and therefore incompatible with our Constitution. It is important not to confuse these things, because being clear about them is what helps us to avoid mistakes.

James Madison thought that the most important test of American freedom would be the ability of our political system to guarantee the rights of minorities without exceptional provisions for their protection. Affirmative action is incompatible with that constitutional design. Whoever calls for affirmative action declares at the same time that that constitutional design has failed and that we can no longer live with our Constitution.

DREW S. DAYS III, associate professor of law, Yale Law School: I want to try to bridge the gap between Brad Reynolds and Ben Hooks. Ben Hooks is, of course, correct that the Civil War amendments were ratified with the principal objective of alleviating discrimination against blacks. But as Brad Reynolds has indicated, the long-term objective was to create a society in which race and color and other characteristics would be irrelevant.

The problem we face today is that we have not achieved either goal. We have not achieved the objective of remedying discrimination, and, therefore, the consideration of race must take place to deal with that problem.

The Congress that ratified the Civil War amendments itself engaged in affirmative action. The Freedmen's Bureau were explicitly designed to benefit blacks, and they used racial classifications. So from a historical standpoint, it is simply incorrect to say that those amendments were designed to frustrate efforts to remedy discrimination against people who had been the victims of injustice.

MR. DALY: To come down to the basic substance of today's debate, the Justice Department is trying to modify existing court orders in some fifty localities so as to limit affirmative action provisions, some of which were developed in response to lawsuits filed by the Justice Department itself in earlier administrations.

In one instance a city administration had agreed to hire one black or Hispanic firefighter for every white firefighter hired and to promote one black or Hispanic firefighter for every four white firefighters promoted. In another, police officers were to be hired at the rate of 35 percent white males, 34 percent minority males, and 31 percent females in each entering class. Mr. Reynolds, why is the Justice Department seeking to change what earlier it sought?

MR. REYNOLDS: Our recent requests that courts modify consent decrees containing quota provisions flow from a 1984 Supreme Court decision that was based on a statutory provision, not on a constitutional provision. That provision was Title VII of the Civil Rights Act of 1964, which outlaws employment discrimination on the basis of race, sex, religion, or ethnic or national origin.

In the Memphis firefighters case—*Firefighters' Local Union 1784* v. *Stotts*—the Supreme Court ruled that that provision forbids the courts from imposing quotas as an element of court-ordered relief. The obligation of the Department of Justice after the Supreme Court had spoken was to return to the courts and ask for a review of outstanding decrees containing quotas, seeking modifications to bring those decrees into line with the command of the Supreme Court. To accomplish that, remedies must be for the benefit of victims of discrimination and must seek to enjoin or stop discriminatory conduct. Affirmative action in the form of outreach and recruitment programs is permissible, but we cannot use discrimination to fight discrimination. Therefore, a court cannot order a quota to try to undo the discrimination that has been charged.

DR. HOOKS: With all due respect, I wish it were that simple. On April 28, 1985, the Court of Appeals for the Eleventh Circuit in the Eglin Airforce Base decision reviewed the same case that Mr. Reynolds referred to and came to exactly the opposite conclusion. One of the eminent jurists of this country, Judge Tuttle, was the senior presiding judge in that case. The fact is that the underlying consent decree was not disturbed by the Supreme Court in the Memphis firefighters case.

That case is read narrowly by most scholars. That is, where the issue of seniority was not covered in the original consent decree, the trial judge was wrong to modify a voluntary consent decree by placing affirmative action above seniority.

Justices O'Connor and Stevens—who concurred to make the majority of six—pointed out that had the underlying decree contained a provision dealing with seniority, the judge could have done what he did. Certainly the Eglin Airforce Base decision, which was just handed down and is the law in the eleventh circuit unless it is overruled, comes to a position diametrically opposed to the one Mr. Reynolds takes.

As the assistant attorney general, Mr. Reynolds has the same right as any other lawyer to interpret the decision. I suspect there are about six or seven hundred thousand of us who will conclude what we wish from it. But it is wrong to imagine that this is what the Supreme Court said, because it did not.

PROFESSOR DAYS: Let me reinforce what Ben Hooks has said. The underlying consent decree in the Memphis firefighters case included a 50 percent hiring goal and a 20 percent promotion goal, and that underlying arrangement was not touched by the Supreme Court. It is also correct that every court that has considered the Justice Department's interpretation of that decision has rejected it.

What I find problematic about the Justice Department's position is not that it takes a very ambitious and broad view of what the Supreme Court decided but that it takes a controversial case whose holding and import are much debated and uses it to seek to overturn consent decrees and voluntary agreements that have been made in scores of communities around the country.

A public official has a responsibility to act only when the law is clear. He should not extrapolate from Supreme Court decisions to overturn approaches that have been taken by prior administrations, both Democratic and Republican.

DR. ALLEN: There is something highly unsatisfactory in our dancing attendance, as a panel or as a people, on eclectic court decisions in various jurisdictions in an attempt to arrive at clarity about fundamental principles. It is true that we need to inquire into court decisions to know what the present state of jurisprudence is. But the ultimate question, of course, is: Does the Constitution tolerate principles such as affirmative action?

We must recognize that we have had court decisions that were radically flawed. We have had them recently, as well as long ago. For instance, we had the *Dred Scott* decision, which in a way produced the very problem that we struggle with now, through its attempt to reinterpret the Declaration of Independence and the U.S. Constitution. Judge Taney's jurisprudence departs from true original intent and would be better called an attempt to establish original *inference*. Original intent properly understood follows the standard laid down in the opinions of *Calder* v. *Bull*. There is no place at all in judicial opinions for original inference.

It was in the context of struggling with the *Dred Scott* decision's reinterpretation of citizenship by analyzing inferences that the Civil Rights amendments after the Civil War came face to face with the question of race. But they did so with this objective: to restore the *status quo ante* before 1857, to get back on the solid ground of the Constitution and the Declaration. We need to have sufficient courage to say on occasion that the courts are wrong and that they are not the last judges of this question.

DR. HOOKS: Dr. Allen, they were not trying to restore the Constitution before 1857. I just read from Article 1, section 2, clause 3, which establishes black folk—they did not call us that, they had a very good way of saying it—as 3/5 of a person. The Thirteenth, Fourteenth, and Fifteenth amendments were not trying to reestablish that state of affairs.

The Thirteenth Amendment was trying to do something specific and new, namely, to abolish slavery. Of the Fourteenth Amendment, you quoted only the part dealing with equal protection and due process. I agree with that, but there are some other very specific things in that amendment. It dealt with people who had taken oaths to other governments—who had been in a state of insurrection. It pointed out how they could qualify to hold office. It is obvious why that constitutional amendment was proposed and ratified.

The Fifteenth Amendment specifically dealt with the right to vote. It said, in effect, that Congress may pass appropriate legislation to effectuate this right. It was almost 100 years before the Voting Rights Act was passed, but the constitutional amendment provided for it.

I like Franklin Roosevelt's statement on March 4th, 1933, that the reason the Constitution has survived is that it is an elastic document. It is very short. It gives the lie to the statement that committees mess up everything—that committee did pretty well. And the thing that makes the Constitution viable is its elasticity, the ability to interpret it. We need only look at the *Dred Scott* decision of the 1850s, *Plessy* v. *Ferguson* in 1897, and *Brown* v. *Board of Education* in 1954 to understand that the Constitution is not static, but is an evolving document designed to deal with the issues as they arise. The worst thing we can do to the Constitution is to pretend that it is dead and has no elasticity.

MR. REYNOLDS: When the Supreme Court speaks, especially in this area, it is probably fair to say that its decisions are always received with some controversy and that lawyers will read the decisions in many different ways. It is well, though, that the Department of Justice and others do not shy away from controversial cases to go after discrimination.

Brown v. *Board of Education*, for that matter, was one of the more controversial decisions handed down by the Court and hardly a model of clarity when it was announced. The Justice Department, in the face of considerable controversy, still went forward into jurisdictions and, on the strength of *Brown*, sought to overturn discriminatory schooling.

What we see today is a decision by the Court that admittedly has generated controversy but has said that it is unlawful and discriminatory to employ quotas and other remedial techniques that rely on race to give preferences and to disadvantage people who are not victims. It is controversial, but it is our department's responsibility, once the Supreme Court has made its pronouncement, to go back to the lower courts in circumstances where we think the discriminatory features exist, to seek to have those features removed.

There has never been a Supreme Court decision, certainly in the Civil Rights area, that has not been controversial. And there has never been an instance in the history of the Civil Rights Division of the Department of Justice where it has not generated controversy through its efforts to ferret out and remove discrimination.

PROFESSOR DAYS: But your reading of the Supreme Court's commands, as you call them, is very selective. The Supreme Court decided in the *Bakke* case that under some circumstances race could be used in admissions decisions. It decided in the *Weber* case that voluntary race-conscious programs could be used for purposes of training blacks and involving them in opportunities from which they have been excluded in the past. And the *Fullilove* decision upheld a statute enacted by Congress that set aside 10 percent for minority contractors in public works programs. How can one look at the *Stotts* decision—which, as Ben Hooks has indicated, deals with statutory interpretation—and view it as the linchpin for a program of overturning decisions made in prior administrations, ignoring *Bakke* and *Weber* and *Fullilove*?

MR. DALY: Let me fill in some details of the cases that you are discussing.

The *Bakke* case is *University of California Regents* v. *Bakke*, 1978. The Court split 5 to 4 over whether the University of California at Davis Medical School's minority set-aside admissions program was constitutional. Justice Powell cast the deciding vote and held that, by making race alone the criterion for admission, Davis acted illegally; but Powell added that if race had been used along with other factors for admissions, the program would have been constitutional.

The Weber case is *United Steel Workers* v. *Weber*, 1979. The Court held that the affirmative action plan worked out between Kaiser Aluminum and its principal employee union, in which half the openings for certain training programs would be reserved for racial minorities, did not violate the prohibition of racial discrimination of the 1964 Civil Rights Act.

In *Fullilove* v. *Klutznick*, 1980, the Public Works Employment Act of 1977 provided that a certain share of federal construction business be set aside for minority contractors. The Court held that congressional use of a racial classification was not unconstitutional in that instance. The opinion held that benevolent racial discrimination by Congress was constitutional as long as it was carefully limited and tailored to remedy some past discrimination.

DR. ALLEN: Those cases, in a sense, only repeat the principle established almost 100 years ago in *Plessy* v. *Ferguson*. There is a change in the application, that is to be conceded, but there is no change in the principle. The principle of that case was that government can have recourse to race or can tolerate discrimination among races in access to public facilities. It was an erroneous principle—one that we have contended against ever since. It is erroneous in the same way, Dr. Hooks, that your historical account is erroneous. I recognize that it is a commonly accepted account, but I am afraid that it is wrong nonetheless.

106

In his debate with Stephen A. Douglas, Abraham Lincoln said that people who try to read the black man out of the Declaration of Independence are blowing out the moral lights among us. And when I speak of returning to the *status quo ante* in understanding the Constitution, I speak of returning to those moral lights that Lincoln sought to resist having blown out. To deny that those moral lights existed is to deny that there is any ground on which to stand to argue in behalf of the rights of black people or any other people.

MR. REYNOLDS: Without getting into too legalistic a discussion, it ought to be said that in the *Fullilove* decision the Court reaffirmed that where you have victims of discrimination, programs can be put in place as long as they are geared to benefit those victims. Congress's program that the Court reviewed in *Fullilove* was one that went directly to victims of discrimination who could prove that they were victims, not unlike the Freedmen's Bureau that Professor Days cited earlier.

The *Weber* case is not a constitutional case but a statutory case. The Court's opinion in that case is very limited and does not suggest any different view of the Constitution from the one that I indicated at the beginning.

In *Bakke* Justice Powell said that we could take race into account in certain circumstances in the educational arena, but as he explained it—and I think this is important—the decision rested essentially on the fact that there was a First Amendment interest competing with a Fourteenth Amendment interest in the educational situation. When those two constitutional rights come head to head, something has to give. In those circumstances, where a balancing must be done to make sure that basic constitutional rights are not infringed, Justice Powell said that some recognition could be given to race but certainly not to the extent that the University of California did.

All these cases still leave the firm conclusion that the Fourteenth Amendment is what the NAACP said it was in its brief in *Brown* v. *Board of Education*: a provision that is colorblind. At that time that was the NAACP's "dedicated belief." I know of no amendment to the Constitution or to the Fourteenth Amendment since the NAACP filed that brief that would explain why its dedicated belief should no longer be the same.

DR. HOOKS: Let me make three points very briefly. First, Dr. Allen, the moral light in the *status quo ante* was the first article of the Constitution, which permitted and perpetuated slavery in this nation for a long, long time. The Thirteenth Amendment was specifically designed to change that.

As for the eloquent argument of Mr. Reynolds, let me make an analogy: No lie will stand long unless it has a little truth mixed in it. That is the cement that keeps it together.

So he can cite what we said about a colorblind society, and he can make of it what he will, but Justice Blackmun in the *Bakke* case dealt most appropriately with this whole question when he pointed out that to reach a colorblind society, we may have to take color and sex into consideration to eliminate inequities, just as we took color and sex into consideration to build those inequities. This problem didn't come about through colorblindness. That did not create this society with all the discrimination, the prejudice, the segregation, the signs that said "Whites only," police departments all over this country, North and South, where no blacks could advance beyond the position of sergeant.

These are facts that have been proved in court time and time again. It is almost silly to have to sit here and talk about them. If anybody wants to say the world is flat, go ahead. But these conditions existed, and the Civil Rights Acts were designed to eradicate them.

Mr. Reynolds is correct when he says the laws were intended to help the victims of discrimination, but let me do with his statement what he did with mine. I maintain, whether they know it or not, and most of us do know it, that all black folk are victims of discrimination. Therefore, we were all intended to be helped by those laws.

The difference is that he only wants to help that one black man who was crazy enough to go to the Memphis fire department when it was white only and ask for a job and get whipped out of there or incarcerated in an insane asylum. To me, it is just not right to say that the only way you can be helped, boy, is to prove that you had enough sense to know that one day we were going to help you and you went down there and made a written application on April 8, 1964. If you bring that here, then we'll help you. Otherwise, sorry.

DR. ALLEN: I want to emphasize that while it is true that the objective for contemporary policy is a colorblind society, a more important objective is a free society. That is to say, we have to get to a colorblind future in a way that preserves the freedom with which we began, and it seems to me shortsighted to deny that this country began with that freedom.

To argue that the Constitution established and perpetuated slavery is a fundamental mistake. When one pulls the Constitution away, one pulls away the structures that through the years gave us our only opportunity to abolish slavery.

I would ask us—if we have to talk about this in a contemporary way—to broaden the conversation to recognize that we are not talking merely about victims and those who suffered but also about those who are guilty of the crime. The problem with affirmative action is that there are a great many grandsons and great-grandsons whom we simply cannot call guilty of any crime, who are nonetheless suffering at the hands of an unjust law. If we are going to talk about the whole society—

DR. HOOKS: Dr. Allen, that's the most ridiculous statement you have made today.

DR. ALLEN: If we are going to talk about the society as a whole, we must find the speech, the language, that addresses the legitimate interests of the whole.

PROFESSOR DAYS: I want to comment on a point that William Allen made about *Plessy* v. *Ferguson*. It is important to distinguish that case and its mode of analysis from what has been happening since *Brown* v. *Board of Education*. The distinction is that *Plessy* v. *Ferguson* was based on a lie. It was based on a false characterization of the society that existed at that time.

The Supreme Court described racially segregated railroad cars as being designed to provide the separation that both races wished. If blacks felt that it was a sign of inferiority, that was just a paranoia that blacks had. That was a lie.

The important thing about *Brown* v. *Board of Education* and the other cases that I mentioned is that they comport with reality—the reality of continued denial of opportunity to blacks, to women, to other racial and ethnic minorities. They are trying to give life to the constitutional document that, as Ben Hooks said, is not written in stone, is not static. Therefore, the objective is a very pragmatic one: how to deal with the continuing deficits and disadvantages that groups suffer in this society that can be traced to slavery and a long period of institutional discrimination.

Professor Allen talks about moral lights and a language for the whole society. I want to know what moral light, what language, he has in mind to deal with that practical problem that we face.

DR. ALLEN: I would love to address that question. You are right that *Plessy* is false on the facts. I do not think, however, it is false to reigning opinion in the society of the time. The Court, in fact, did the same thing that it did in *Brown*. It asked itself, How do people think about these things? What are their opinions?

I think the Court's statement of the opinions that prevailed then was, indeed, correct, just as *Brown* v. *Board of Education*, using sociological analyses and similar ways of collecting public opinion, was more or less a reflection of its time. But common opinion is not the same thing as true principle, and the errors in *Plessy* have to do with principles, not with the common opinions of the time. The true language, as I said, is the language of a free society—a language that recognizes and honors in citizens an ambition to merit and claim the honors of their society. Freedom and equality seen through an exclusive focus on the material conditions of life are only slavery refined by rhetoric. At the same time, the surest means to enhance a people's material condition is to confirm their moral and political capacity, leaving the rest to them. That was the gamble of the Founding, which we can see to have been proved in the event. The moral light—the equality of the Declaration—is the view that men can govern themselves. They revert to law for protection, but they and not the government are the free agents. The law should be as a hired gun, following the individual's lead, not as an authoritarian tutor or overseer.

On Professor Days's general question—what can we do to achieve desegregation?—there is a great paradox in what affirmative action seeks to do. Mostly it asks the government to intervene in markets—primarily labor markets—although it asks other things too, to produce a certain result. But it is asking the government to undo what the government itself did, through the National Industrial Recovery Act and the National Labor Relations Act. Those acts, in effect, gave local unions the power to discriminate and restrict entry of blacks and others into the labor market.

During all the years since those acts were passed, those who were harmed by that policy had the opportunity to call it what it was. But they chose instead to play along with the labor movement and sustain the edifice of discrimination.

MR. REYNOLDS: I agree with Drew Days that *Plessy* was grounded in a lie, and Justice Harlan's eloquent dissent identified the lie as the majority's reading of the Constitution as being other than colorblind. That dissent became the majority view, in *Brown* and subsequent cases, that we have a colorblind document. I don't agree that if we disengage ourselves from quota remedies, we are somehow leaving untouched or unattended the problem of discrimination and that there is no way to remedy that discrimination.

I agree with Dr. Hooks that discrimination continues in this country and that we cannot rest until we have dealt to the fullest with the effects of past discrimination. But there are ways to do it that do not

110

buy into the same kind of evil that we condemn when we condemn the evil of discrimination. For the past four years we have used affirmative action in the form of an outreach and recruitment program that goes into communities to find members of minorities and women who are qualified and interested in jobs and brings them into the applicant pool. Employers then select people for hiring or promotion on a nondiscriminatory basis. If you want to look at results, that kind of race-neutral regime has brought more members of minorities and more women into the public work force where we have enforcement responsibility, more than we would expect if the remedy were tied to some kind of artificial quota.

So it can be done. These jurisdictions are all telling us, when we go in now after *Stotts*, "We want to hire increased numbers of minorities and women. We're out looking for them. We're trying to do right by everybody in equal opportunities." That is the climate today. We don't have a climate where jurisdictions are digging in their heels against the effort to bring minorities and women into the work force. With that kind of climate and that kind of race-neutral regime, we can expect better results than with programs tied to an artificial number.

DR. HOOKS: Let me bring up two cases that arose in Alabama, one in 1970, one in 1972. The NAACP filed *NAACP* v. *Allen* because in 1972, after thirty-seven years of existence, the Alabama highway patrol had never hired a single black patrolman. Not one. We had exhausted all our administrative remedies.

Finally we went to court seeking to have black patrolmen added to the Alabama highway patrol. In that protracted litigation Alabama's answer was always just what Mr. Reynolds has talked about: "We've recruited. We've sought. We have advertised in the *Black Dispatch*. Get the NAACP and the Urban League and the SCLC to give us names. We've done all we know how to do and nothing has worked." Finally Judge Frank Johnson, having been exasperated by their failure to hire a single black, directed that henceforth they hire one black applicant for every white applicant.

Now, around the time the *Allen* suit was filed, a suit was also filed against all the departments of the Alabama state government for failure to hire black applicants. But in that case, *U.S.* v. *Frazer*, the judge did not require any goals to be met. And a strange thing happened. After the passage of a few months—a few years, in fact—more black people were hired by the Alabama highway patrol than by all the seventy-five other departments of the state government put together. In one case they had a goal to meet, which was one black applicant for every white applicant, and in the other case they were simply told to recruit. Oh, they had plans—I suspect that the plans to recruit would fill this room.

It did not work then, and, Mr. Reynolds, I suggest to you very respectfully that it will not work today. I have listened to Mayor Hudnut of Indianapolis, Mayor Washington of Chicago, Mayor Bradley of Los Angeles, Mayor Schaefer of Baltimore, and they have all said the same thing. The plans they have now are working and are producing results and in a way that they think is satisfactory. I think Mayor Hudnut used that old expression: if it ain't broke, don't fix it.

This country is in favor of goals and timetables. We don't say to Detroit, "We hope that by January 1, 1986, you will produce a fleet of cars that will get 32 miles to the gallon. Now, we're not going to do anything to you if you don't do it, but try, experiment. Get some George Washington Carvers and Thomas Edisons. Put them out there in the laboratory. Let them work." No, Congress said to them, "By January 1, 1986, you will have a fleet of cars that gets that mileage, and if you don't, you're going to be fined several million dollars a year." They had a penalty attached to it.

When Congress enacted the 55-mile-an-hour limit, it didn't say, "You're a great patriotic people. Study the impact theory. See how many people get killed." No, it said, on a certain day if you go over 55, you're subject to arrest. I maintain that a law has to have some penalties, some deterrent value, to work.

What we are saying to you, Mr. Reynolds, is that if you firmly, sincerely believe what you say, I can give you a number of jurisdictions that are not doing anything. I suggest you go there and try working with them—virgin, clean territory. [Laughter.] Work with them your way and see if they won't do better, and let those that are now working with goals go along as they are. Then in ten years let's go back and see what you have accomplished voluntarily and what we have accomplished with a goal, and I think you'll agree with me.

DR. ALLEN: Let me just say a word about that, if I may, Dr. Hooks, because I think no one is suggesting that there isn't a call for an active and energetic Justice Department in the civil rights area. I can think of many ways in which its activity can continue and expand consistently with the Constitution. But the real question embedded in your Alabama examples is not whether a plan works or not but whether it is right.

I can name several other plans that would work very well and would give us a complete peppering of the whole society. The question is, may we do those things? Ought we to do them? And the point is, of course, that we oughtn't to do them because they are inconsistent with the Constitution.

DR. HOOKS: Professor Allen. You keep raising this question of right and wrong, and you become so moral and you take such high ground—

DR. ALLEN: Thank you.

DR. HOOKS: —and it makes me look like a knave or a fool.

DR. ALLEN: No, I don't think you look a fool.

DR. HOOKS: With all due respect, your objections don't have any practicality to them, as far as I'm concerned. You say, Is it right? Who is the judge of right? I'm a Christian, and in my Judeo-Christian heritage only God can decide right; I don't ascribe that power to any of us sitting here.

DR. ALLEN: I think we, the people, can decide that.

DR. HOOKS: Let me just get this on the table. This is a great country, and it is great specifically because the Constitution is a great document, and it is a great document because of its elasticity.

Acts have been passed that the Supreme Court has held to be unconstitutional, and I accept that whether I like the results or not. I accept the fact that over this long stretch of time, coming from horses and buggies to people landing on the moon, this Constitution has not become outdated or outmoded. It is a brilliant, beautiful document, and I glory in those who wrote it. But I don't know by what constitutional authority you decide what is right and what is wrong.

I simply said that we had a problem, and in one instance the court tried two different approaches to desegregation in the same state. One achieved results, and one did not, and, while my Judeo-Christian heritage on rightness and wrongness is still applicable, all I can deal with as a lawyer is the pragmatic results.

Since I don't often have a chance to talk with Mr. Reynolds, I am asking him now to think about what I said. [Laughter.]

PROFESSOR DAYS: I have several points to make. First, I think we all agree that goals and timetables, with the explicit use of race or sex as criteria, are not appropriate in every circumstance. There is a range of remedies that we can use to deal with specific problems, and yet we talk about goals, timetables, and quotas as though they were used in every instance to respond to quite different situations.

Second, goals, timetables, and other numerical measurements were instituted because of the experience that prior administrations had had with good faith efforts, as Dr. Hooks noted. Year after year passed and nothing changed. Finally the courts and administrative agencies said, "We're going to have to do something about this. We've had enough of your good faith. Where is the change? Where are the results? Where are the jobs for blacks or for women or Hispanics?" It was out of frustration that these techniques were developed. They are regarded as interim measures.

You talk about "equality of result." I don't think that is a correct characterization of the approaches that have been used. They are interim measures to bring an institution to the point where the society can regard it as capable of acting in a colorblind and nondiscriminatory fashion.

If an employment situation is all white or all male, the likelihood is, given the years of exclusion of certain groups, that the institution will continue to function in exclusionary ways. The way to open up that institution, to give the sense that it really is committed to equality of opportunity, is to force some change not in the theory but in the practice of that institution.

These approaches have worked. Brad Reynolds can cite his studies and I can cite mine, but the truth is that affirmative action in the use of goals and timetables has produced results. Studies have shown what happened in the absence of goals and timetables and what happened where they were available.

Finally, the cases that have been the subject of so much controversy recently were the result of a conviction, which one can find in congressional hearings and testimony and debates, that what Congress had in mind was not protracted litigation, not contention, not conflict, but an attempt to solve these very difficult problems voluntarily.

When we in the Carter administration went into a jurisdiction to look at an all-white police department or an all-white fire department, we developed enough evidence to win a case of employment discrimination. Nonetheless, we went to those jurisdictions and said, "Would you rather work this out amicably or would you like to fight? Because if you want to fight, we think we're going to beat you, and perhaps the results will be more difficult for you than resolving this voluntarily."

Looking at what has happened in recent months, I have begun to think that my predecessors and I were remiss in this regard. What we should have done was nail them to the wall and establish who all the victims of discrimination were in those police departments and

114

fire departments, so that when this administration came along, they would be actual names, instead of anonymous people buried in the graveyards of America.

MR. REYNOLDS: On the higher plain of right versus wrong—and I hesitate to speak to this—I think I can say with some degree of assurance that all of us around this table agree that discrimination on account of race is simply wrong. To me a quota or a goal or a timetable or any other numerical device that assigns a preference to one person and disadvantages another because of race is discrimination itself and is wrong, because it is not dealing in either case with the victims of discrimination.

Whether such a device has worked is not, I think, to be measured by how many individuals have come into a work force by reason of its use. If a remedy discriminates, it is not moving us in a direction that will eliminate discrimination. And when you call it an interim measure, it's hard for me to see where the measure suddenly ceases. Where do we disengage? At what point do we have a balanced work force? If we remove whatever governmental hand has accomplished that and things start sliding out of equipoise, what do we do then?

I think it is a mistake to say that something has worked by looking at numerical balance. It works if we eliminate discrimination. That is what we are about. That is what we want to do. We want to get rid of discrimination in this country. I don't see us eliminating discrimination by buying into a remedial device that subscribes to and encourages discrimination on the basis of race and that says it's only an interim measure, while at the same time it reinforces over and over again the evil we want to get behind us.

Those who say, as Justice Blackmun said, that we need to use race to get beyond racism should recall that we don't use alcohol to get beyond alcoholism. It doesn't make much sense to buy into the very evil that we have said over and over again around this table is contemptible and that we condemn outright and unequivocally.

MR. DALY: Now it is time for the first question from the audience.

HYMAN BOOKBINDER, American Jewish Committee: All the panel members seem to be using words interchangeably that ought not to be considered interchangeable. The words "affirmative action," "goals," and "quotas" mean different things.

I am terribly disturbed that the Reagan administration has sought to outlaw not only quotas—quotas that may conceivably lead to what is called reverse discrimination—but the system of goals as well. Goals are different from quotas, contain no dangers, and have worked in government employment and other places. Is it not true that we can have a system of goals and timetables that does not have the obnoxious features of quotas?

MR. REYNOLDS: I do think it is true, Mr. Bookbinder, that the debate on this subject has suffered because the terms used are not well defined. Affirmative action as it was traditionally understood in the civil rights arena referred solely to the race-neutral affirmative outreach and recruitment programs put in place in the early 1960s. When I speak of affirmative action, that is how I understand it, and that seems to me the only legitimate definition of the term.

Quotas are rigid or inflexible numbers defined by race, sex, or national origin that employers must reach. They run afoul of the constitutional principles of equal opportunity and neutrality.

The term "goals" has been used variously by people on both sides of the debate. In my view goals are permissible as long as they do not in any way condone preference by race or gender or ethnic origin or religion. But if the operation of a goal is to afford a benefit—no matter how small—to any individual because of immutable characteristics it is no different from a quota. It matters not what label we use; if a quota, a goal, a preference, a set-aside, or any other numerical device assigns a benefit by reason of an immutable characteristic, it runs afoul of constitutional principle and of Title VII.

DR. HOOKS: There is a vast difference between the use of a quota and the use of a goal. We've always known what a quota was. It was an absolute ceiling above which one could not rise, such as three seats for some racial group in the medical school, five positions on the police department, and no more. The NAACP historically is on record as being absolutely opposed to the use of rigid quotas.

Affirmative action, however, was designed to do at least one thing in addition to what Mr. Reynolds has said. At some point there had to be some result. Why would we spend all this time in Congress and all this money just to end up with a process that brought about no results?

This awareness evolved from a long list of cases, struggles, and trials all over this country. That is the greatness of our country and of our Constitution, that they evolve. In the course of that evolution, primarily white judges of varied backgrounds, conservative and liberal, came to similar conclusions in different places: that we must establish goals and timetables if the law is to have any effect.

Mr. Days was correct when he said it would have been far better, in hindsight, to nail the people to the wall and prove job discrimination instead of pursuing consent decrees. A consent decree obviously shortcuts some things; everybody agrees it happened, so that it's not necessary to go through all the gory details. Let's admit it and get it over with. But we're stuck now with incomplete records; so the Reagan Justice Department can maintain that there were no victims.

On that question of victims, that is such a terribly difficult and dangerous word to deal with. When I went into the Army, every general save one, B.O. Davis, was white. Now we have quite a few black generals. If there is one black general or one woman general, I don't want to hear that every white colonel is a victim because he's not a general too. There is a kind of subliminal arrogance involved in thinking that no women or blacks ever get to be generals unless they get preferential treatment—that standing on level ground, white males will always have every good job in the country.

Suppose the Memphis police department had 700 policemen in 1949, all white and all male, and that in 1985 some of the 700 police are black and some are female. Clearly, some white male is a victim.

A victim of what? A victim of equality, fairness, and equity. The supposition is that if somehow we just didn't have to deal with women, if they weren't so pushy and obnoxious, if they didn't want to have good jobs, by God, we'd still have 700 white males. If black folk would just go back to doing what they were doing before the Civil Rights Act and apply and get turned down, we would have this thing licked, and no white males would be discriminated against.

DR. ALLEN: I have a deep appreciation for Dr. Hooks's struggle. I am reminded of Abraham Lincoln in the debate with Stephen A. Douglas. Douglas among others tried to read blacks out of the Declaration of Independence. To do so, he came up with a formula that the Declaration was written only for white Anglo-Saxons. Lincoln would run through the Midwest, which was then heavily populated by immigrants who were not Anglo-Saxons, reminding them what that formula meant for them.

When we try to define things as nebulous as race and heritage, we are going to have those kinds of problems. Ultimately, however, we are not concerned with which individuals are in or out. We are concerned with what is the legitimate power of the state, of the government. That is the question we are talking about.

I frankly am sometimes just driven to distraction by this. When I served on a school board, we talked constantly about goals, timetables, quotas, affirmative action, guidelines, objectives. I kept saying to people, "Look, why can't you just let people go to school?" They kept coming back, insisting we had to pepper the whole district with all these little faces. Finally I got so exasperated that I said, "Look, I want you people to understand something. There ain't enough of us to go around for every white man to own one." [Laughter.]

PROFESSOR DAYS: That is a humorous story about a very sad situation.

On this question of definition, I find it almost impossible, given the fragility of words, to make meaningful distinctions among those terms. Certainly we don't want to replicate or reproduce a quota in this society ever again. I know of no affirmative action program, no remedial measure, that even comes close to the quotas that kept Jews in particular out of colleges and universities, not only in the United States but around the world.

I find it helpful to look at the nature of the problem and try to understand the degree to which the remedy is designed to address that problem. Sometimes, as I said earlier, aggressive recruitment may be the way to go.

In other situations we may have to use goals and timetables. It may be a situation like the Alabama state police case, where the court says, "You have had enough time to engage in good faith efforts. From now on until you reach a certain level, you are going to have to hire one black for every white that you hire." But the understanding is that this is going to end at some point.

There may be some instances in which these objectives become hard and fast and employers or school boards use them irrespective of considerations of quality or merit, but I think that is the exception. I'm not denying that there are such instances, and I would abhor them. But in the vast majority of situations this process simply forces an employer or a school board to bring in people who are qualified— who are out there and simply couldn't be found until the court or an administrative agency said, "You've got to look and come back with something."

Where there's a demonstrable indication of a good faith effort to find and hire or admit, I know of no court that has insisted, nevertheless, that a certain number be reached. As we've been saying all along, this is a pragmatic process designed to produce results that make sense, not to create a situation that is absurd.

FRANK MATTHEWS, George Mason University, publisher of *Black Issues in Higher Education*: Would Professor Days please comment on the ironic contrast between the original *DeFunis* case, which the court declared moot, and the *Stotts* decision, in which the minority opinion also argued that the issue was moot? What was the difference between those two cases?

MR. DALY: Will you please summarize the two cases?

PROFESSOR DAYS: *DeFunis* was a predecessor to the *Bakke* case, except that it never happened. The Supreme Court agreed to hear a case in which a white student at the University of Washington Law School challenged an affirmative action plan and admissions program for minority students. The Court ultimately dismissed the case as moot since DeFunis had been admitted to the law school and was about to graduate, so that there was no live controversy for the Court to resolve.

In the *Stotts* case, there was a similar argument that, to the extent that some harm had been done to the laid-off white firefighters, that harm had passed because they had been restored to their positions in the meantime, so that it was insignificant as a matter of law. The dissenters in *Stotts* suggested that the Supreme Court was reaching out to decide the case, even though there was evidence that the matter had been taken care of by the passage of time.

While lawyers can debate whether that was a fair action on the part of the Supreme Court, your question suggests something else about that case. The Supreme Court, the media, and the public debate have depicted it as a case in which less qualified junior black firefighters were kept on the job while senior and more qualified white firefighters were laid off. But the plan at issue in *Stotts* was, in fact, a reverse alphabetical layoff plan. The Memphis fire department had decided that if layoffs occurred, they would be in reverse alphabetical order among persons equally qualified.

The black and white firefighters in the *Stotts* case had the same seniority dates and were equally qualified to do the job. But the three whites had names that began with A, D, and D, whereas the blacks had names that began with H, J, and J. Under the terms of the seniority plan, the blacks should have been laid off.

What the trial court said was that a fire department that had agreed to bring in blacks who claimed they had been victims of discrimination should not be laying off blacks disproportionately. Yet, as I say, the public debate over *Stotts* characterizes it as a case in which job qualifications were at issue. In too many instances the public debate about quotas and goals fails to acknowledge the complexity of the issues and the degree to which there is quite a bit of justice on both sides.

MR. REYNOLDS: Precisely because seniority was so tangential an aspect of *Stotts*, the Court's opinion is much more important for what it implies about preferential treatment in all contexts, whether layoffs or hiring or promotions. The Court in *Stotts* was not confining its decision to seniority but was looking to what Title VII did or did not authorize the courts to do.

The Supreme Court went through passage after passage of the legislative history of Title VII. It found that the sponsors of that legislation on both sides of the aisle repeatedly said that Title VII does not tolerate the use of quotas and the use of preferences based on race. The Court said in *Stotts* that those features must be removed from any remedy of an employment discrimination case that advantages somebody and disadvantages another solely because of race.

DR. HOOKS: The fact remains, however, that the underlying consent decree in the *Stotts* case was not overruled by the Supreme Court. So what is clear to Mr. Reynolds and the Justice Department is not clear to the majority of lawyers, to the circuit courts who have heard it since that time, to the mayors, or to the municipalities who have refused to yield to it.

RANDALL RADER, Senate Judiciary Committee: In the landmark case *Brown* v. *Board of Education* it was held that a student may not be deprived of the right to attend his neighborhood school solely on the basis of race, a very laudable goal. Now, a few decades later, we find courts requiring students to be taken out of their neighborhood schools on the basis of their race and bused clear across town to attend distant schools with some damage to their education.

I am a parent with two black children and two white children. I would find it very offensive if one of my children who is black were bused to a different school from the one her white sister attends or vice versa. Is not the race-conscious remedy of mandatory busing violative of the principle set down in *Brown*, that students should not be assigned to schools on the basis of race?

DR. ALLEN: The difficulty in answering your question has to do with problems inherent in *Brown*. I certainly agree that *Brown* achieved a remarkable political transition in the country. That is to say, it made apparent to all of us a general commitment to achieve a colorblind society and a fully integrated society.

I cannot concur, however, that the opinion in *Brown* was as free of taint as you suggest it is. It did not, in my reading, completely overturn *Plessy* v. *Ferguson*. *Brown*, in fact, backed away from simply adopting Justice Harlan's dissent in *Plessy*. And I think the reason it backed away is that there was some hesitation to be without a race-conscious remedy, though now, of course, for putatively positive reasons.

MR. DALY: Summarize the *Plessy* case, please.

DR. ALLEN: In the 1896 case, *Plessy* v. *Ferguson*, the issue was transportation in railroad cars and segregation. The Court, in judging the case, was asked to read the Fourteenth Amendment as requiring absolute access for blacks and others to all public facilities and, indeed, by implication to private facilities engaged in interstate commerce. The Court reasoned that the mores, the habits, the customs of the people would not sustain government-imposed integration and that all the Constitution really called for was, in the famous phrase from that case, separate but equal facilities.

Shortly after *Plessy* the separate but equal provision came to be applied broadly in cases of public education—an important area at the time, because in the District of Columbia and elsewhere, there were numerous efforts to integrate schools. So we lived from *Plessy* to *Brown* on the principle of separate but equal. That position was based on a presumed fact, namely, that you could separate and still make equal.

Brown looked at the facts and said separate is not equal. It even said separate is inherently not equal, but it didn't go beyond that to say race consciousness in itself is unconstitutional. It stopped at simply reading the facts and saying that because the separateness we see is not equal, we can no longer support it. In principle, then, the constitutional rule in our country would still be that if we had the technology to generate equal conditions, we could segregate people any way we wanted.

DR. HOOKS: It is always interesting to me that while more than 50 percent of all American schoolchildren are bused each and every day, all the furor is about the 4 percent who are bused for purposes of racial desegregation. I have never heard anybody ask why kids are bused 30 miles in Montana or why they are bused to private schools all over the South, because everybody understands why that happens.

In *Swann* v. *Mecklenberg*, one of the early cases dealing with busing, the county had 900 buses and spent $14 million a year to bus 110,000 kids. This was in 1971, seventeen years after the *Brown* decision. The Court held that if they could spend $14 million and use all those buses to keep segregation intact they could use the same buses and the same amount of money to make the school system desegregated.

I can understand that all of us have personal problems with some of the things that happen in the local school system, like compulsory school attendance, busing, where they build a school, or why they close a school. But I really cannot deal with personal situations. All I can deal with is trying to meet the mandate of *Brown*, and that is that separate but equal is inherently unconstitutional. After thirty-one years the country still has a majority of segregated systems, and busing is only one of the many remedies that have been used to try to fulfill that mandate.

PROFESSOR DAYS: I understand your concern. I have two children and they ride buses to public schools. I am happy about that because I like what's at the end of the bus ride. Busing is as American as the little red schoolhouse.

The problem has been that neighborhood schools have often been defined by race, to segregate schools. I've been involved in a number of school desegregation cases in which the "neighborhood" went from the center of town out into the country to keep white children together in a segregated school. The same thing was true for blacks.

There was an effort in the early days after *Brown* to allow students freedom of choice to decide whether they were gong to remain in segregated quasi-neighborhood schools or transfer to schools that were, in fact, closer to their homes than the schools to which they had been assigned under segregation. What the courts found and what blacks learned very quickly was that exercising this freedom of choice was about as foolhardy as going to the Memphis fire department to apply for a job during the time when blacks simply were not going to be hired.

Therefore, the courts took the position that something had to be changed. It's referred to as equality of results, but I think it's something other than that. It is a response to discrimination. I would hope that at some point in our history we would develop neighborhoods that were, in fact, reflective of freedom of choice, of personal decisions, and not the manifestations of deep-seated racism.

MR. REYNOLDS: Mr. Rader's valid question is, Why are race-conscious quota remedies tolerable as a constitutional matter in the school desegregation context but intolerable in the employment context? The answer is that all the children in a de jure segregated school district are victims, and it is constitutionally permissible to use a race-conscious remedy to make the victims whole.

What the Court did in *Swann* and subsequent cases was to experiment with a remedy of forced busing in an effort to make those victims whole by desegregating the system. What fell through the cracks is the other element of *Brown*, that of attending to the educational needs of the children in the system.

One of the reasons this administration has had so much of a problem with court-ordered busing is that it turns essentially one-race schools into one-race school districts and pays little, if any, attention to the educational needs of the children in those districts. That is why we have sought to fashion an alternative remedy that leans heavily on magnet schools and does not rely on forced busing.

The difficulty with a quota is that it goes well beyond making the victims whole to benefit those who are not victims, who were not even in the work force or were in grade school when the discrimination went on. When they come to the door, the employer, because of a quota and their race, has to open the door to that contingent or group.

The mischief of that situation really should cause us to look over our shoulder at *Plessy*, because to me separate employment lists that are supposed to translate into equal results are very close to the principle of separate but equal in *Plessy* v. *Ferguson*.

DR. HOOKS: But if the government decides to eliminate all references to race and to sex, we have the perfect world for those who are entrenched in positions of authority and power.

MR. REYNOLDS: But that does not eliminate litigation.

DR. HOOKS: There is no way to measure whether or not we are making ascertainable progress. And it looks as if we are being blind to history. We're not living in a fantasy land or a perfect world. We're living in a world of imperfect beings where segregation and discrimination were for a long time a way of life, where there were de jure and de facto measures that kept certain people back.

As Judy Goldsmith of the National Organization for Women so eloquently put it, if it took hundreds of years to get here, we're not going to eliminate it in twenty years. We've had the civil rights laws, one of them passed in 1964, EEOC in 1967. We've been struggling in a marvelous way. As a black person I have a lot to complain about, but one thing I've been proud of is the struggle that we have made— black and white, male and female together—to overcome some of these historical barriers.

We've had differences—friends have fallen out sometimes—and we've made new allies. But it has been a steady march to make this thing happen.

To start talking now about colorblindness and sex blindness, as if they are new things just discovered, and put such sanctity on them, will not lead us to the elimination of historical discrimination.

DR. ALLEN: It is far from the case that colorblindness has just been discovered. Between roughly 1946 and the *Bakke* decision no dissenting opinion was more frequently cited than the Harlan opinion in *Plessy*. It showed up in sixty-four cases, and it has shown up frequently since then and, of course, before. This is not new. It is the story of America.

Let me give you an example of how we may come to the defense of minorities without race-conscious remedies. During the debate over the Reconstruction amendments, one of the grave concerns was that in many southern communities at that time the sheriff would secure a warrant to search and seize people's weapons. After the weapons were taken, the Klan would come back in the dead of night, when people were defenseless, to assault them. It happened on a very wide scale. Congress was deeply concerned to enforce the Second Amendment to the Constitution, (the right of the people to keep arms) to prevent that from happening, and they got involved. That is not race conscious. That is going to the roots of the document itself, that is responding to people's needs.

Therefore, it is wrong to suggest that goals, quotas, and timetables are the only recourse. The American Constitution is a resilient, rich, and expansive document, not evolving but, as all the founders said, there to serve us as long as we are worthy of it.

WALTER WILLIAMS, George Mason University: In reaching what we all agree should be the objective of equality, how effective is it to keep stressing goals and timetables in employment and college admissions while allowing the public schools to destroy black education on a day-to-day basis, as evidenced by 47 percent illiteracy among black seventeen-year-olds and black failure rates on SAT scores, GRE scores, and LSAT scores? After you answer that, I have a particular question for Benjamin Hooks since he has said so many complimentary things about President Reagan. Much of affirmative action is based on Executive Order 11246. Now, President Reagan can rescind that order with a stroke of a pen. Would you care to speculate on why he does not?

DR. HOOKS: I'd like to think, happily, that Mr. Reagan realizes that he is president of all the people and that that executive order is necessary and that he is going to keep it in place, and I respect and admire him for doing it.

MR. REYNOLDS: As to your general question, Mr. Williams, I think that the point is exceedingly well taken. One of the things that has impressed me most since I've been in this job is the overreliance on the Civil Rights Act of 1964 and its companion laws to cure all the ills that may or may not be attributable to discrimination in this country.

Public education is a good example. We attend much less to many of the problems that face all students and are content instead to suggest that if we can somehow make the numbers work on racial balance, we won't need to worry too much about the rest of the educational process. But when a young person gets up to the employment door without a good education because of that neglect, there may be some reason other than employment discrimination why he is not chosen.

We have to take a hard look at exactly how much baggage we're going to heap on the shoulders of the Civil Rights Acts. Many of the core problems come along much earlier in the process, before people ever get to the employment door, and they are not addressed in any way by getting the numbers in the work force to look right.

PROFESSOR DAYS: I think it is an important point also, but it is not an either-or situation. I don't know anyone who really embraces goals and timetables as Brad Reynolds describes them as the solution to the problem.

It was not the Carter administration or prior administrations that cut educational funds 25 percent or raised questions about Title I, a program that has been shown to be effective in bringing poor children up to the educational level where they ought to be. Certainly there must be educational quality. But what do we do while we wait for the millennium? One of the things about this society has been that we pitch in and try to deal with the world as we find it and deal with as much of the problem as we can now while looking to long-term and institutional solutions.

I certainly hope that in the next century we're not still talking about goals and timetables throughout the society, that we really have made some advances. But I must admit that, looking at the situation today, I am somewhat depressed at the outlook.

GAYLE BRADLEY STARKES, Appalachian Regional Commission: I would like Professor Allen to clarify his opinion that the Constitution was for everyone and did not perpetuate slavery before the Reconstruction amendments. When the Constitution was written and for some time thereafter, black people were indeed in slavery.

Would he also explain what he means by moral lights and what mechanism he would substitute for affirmative action?

DR. ALLEN: Let me start with the second question. "Moral lights" was Abraham Lincoln's own phrase. He was referring to the influence of the principle stated in the Declaration of Independence that all men are created equal, that they are endowed by their creator with certain rights. Those are moral lights in the deepest sense, not just a philosophical gloss. They are moral lights in the sense that the life of the people of this country has been framed by those principles. Our lives are governed by those principles.

That leads to the answer to your first question about the Constitution. But let me just take a moment to address a pervasive misunderstanding of this country's history—one we genuinely need to struggle with if we are ever going to respond to our past in a way that does justice to the Constitution. Yes, slavery existed at the time of the adoption of the Constitution. It existed before. It existed afterward. But we have to recognize that the founders, although slavery continued to exist, did not place a stamp of approval on it.

They went as far as they could, in fact, toward placing a stamp of disapproval on it. None of the provisions of the Constitution, including the three-fifths clause to which Dr. Hooks incorrectly referred, ever mention the word "slave." They said they intentionally wanted to avoid staining the document with that word because they looked to the day when slavery would be gone from this country. Nor does the Constitution refer to a black as three-fifths of a person. It refers instead to three-fifths of the aggregate number of all other persons.

The very first constitutional debate in the House of Representatives was a debate over slavery. In that debate it was James Madison, the father of the Constitution, who was the most eloquent of all in saying that ultimately he and his allies hoped to rid the country of this sin, this stain of slavery.

The question has been with us ever since the beginning. It is with us now, obviously, and we continue to live with its consequences. We continually have to make decisions in light of the possibilities that exist for us. But we must understand those possibilities in a historical context that shows slavery, in effect, being driven out by the guiding principles of the nation, of the Constitution.

The end of slavery, the Civil War, the Reconstruction amendments did not come about simply because at a certain moment in history there was a fantastic revelation and what was all dark suddenly turned bright and shiny. It came about because the educative effect of these principles was there working, fermenting to produce the reaction that

126

not only would abolish slavery but would lead us all ultimately to adopt the principles of the American founding as our own and make possible a genuine national life in which we forget about group rights and instead talk about the rights of individual human beings.

MR. DALY: This concludes another public policy forum presented by the American Enterprise Institute for Public Policy Research. On behalf of AEI, our hearty thanks to the distinguished and expert panelists, Professor William B. Allen, the Honorable Wm. Bradford Reynolds, Dr. Benjamin L. Hooks, and the Honorable Drew S. Days III, and also to our guests and experts in the audience for their participation.

5

How Should We Interpret the Constitution?

Walter Berns
Robert A. Goldwin
Abner Mikva
Laurence Tribe
J. Clifford Wallace

R OBERT A. GOLDWIN, director of constitutional studies of the American Enterprise Institute: This public policy forum, one of a series presented by the American Enterprise Institute, examines an issue that presidents, legislators, judges, and thoughtful citizens have struggled with from the beginning of our republic: How can we apply our Constitution to the constantly new circumstances, policies, and aspirations of this ever-changing nation? To help us understand this issue we have a distinguished and expert panel of judges and scholars.

Laurence Tribe, the Ralph Tyler Professor of Constitutional Law at Harvard Law School, is the author of many books and articles, including *Constitutional Choices, God Save This Honorable Court,* and the widely used textbook, *American Constitutional Law.*

Circuit Judge Abner J. Mikva, who serves on the U.S. Court of Appeals for the District of Columbia, was elected five times to the U.S. House of Representatives as a Democratic congressman from Illinois.

Circuit Judge J. Clifford Wallace, who serves on the U.S. Court of Appeals for the Ninth Circuit, was a U.S. District Judge for the Southern District of California.

Finally, Walter Berns is the John M. Olin University Professor at Georgetown University and an adjunct scholar at the American Enterprise Institute. A political scientist, Professor Berns is also the author of many books and articles, including *In Defense of Liberal Democracy,* and the soon to be published *Taking the Constitution Seriously.*

Recently, the nation witnessed an unusual public exchange of views on this issue of how to interpret the Constitution, with the attorney general of the United States on one side of the argument and a sitting justice of the Supreme Court on the other.

Speaking before the American Bar Association, Attorney General Edwin Meese III argued that the only legitimate way for courts to interpret the Constitution is to be guided by the original intention of those who wrote and ratified the document. Judges who depart from that standard of interpretation, he warned, substitute their own personal whim for the will of the American people. When that happens, he said, "the idea of democracy has suffered [and] the permanence of the Constitution has been weakened. A constitution that is viewed as only what the judges say it is, is no longer a Constitution in the true sense."

Associate Justice William J. Brennan soon after expressed a sharply different view of this jurisprudence of original intention. In a speech at Georgetown University, he argued, "It is arrogant to pretend that from our vantage we can gauge accurately the intent of the framers. . . . Typically, all that can be gleaned is that the framers themselves did not agree . . . and hid their differences in cloaks of generality. . . . Those who would restrict claims of right to the values of 1789 specifically articulated in the Constitution, turn a blind eye to social progress and eschew adaptation of overarching principles to changes of social circumstances."

These two statements bracket the problem of how to read and apply the Constitution when we need its guidance in making laws, executing the laws, or deciding legal controversies. Mr. Meese and Justice Brennan point out clearly and forcefully the difficulties and the dangers.

On one side, if we disregard the intention of the authors, that may lead us to disregard the text, the words, and the provisions of the Constitution and what they were intended to mean. What then, other than the personal preferences of the judges, will be the law? As Mr. Meese would ask, If the Constitution is only what the judges say it is, is there a Constitution?

On the other side, Justice Brennan points to difficulties with the attempt to find the original intent of the framers, who disagreed on much in the Constitution, while it was being written and subsequently. And even if the original intention can be known, he asks, can we allow ourselves to be held back by the views of a time long gone? Must we not read the Constitution in a way that permits social progress in accord with the times?

According to these two opposing views, if we follow the lead of the attorney general, we have a sense of constitutional stability but the danger that an eighteenth-century document might prevent twentieth-century social progress. And if we follow Justice Brennan's lead, social and political change is facilitated but at the risk of lawmaking by the courts—constitutional amendment not by the amending process but by judges.

Now, with the problem thus before us, gentlemen, I put the same

132

question to each of you and ask, What is your answer: How should we interpret the Constitution?

ABNER J. MIKVA, Judge, U.S. Court of Appeals: At the risk of trying to combine the uncombinable neither Justice Brennan nor Attorney General Meese said what the other said he said. Justice Brennan never said that the Constitution is only what the judges say it is, and Attorney General Meese doesn't really want to write every *S* like an *F*, and insist that the Constitution can only mean what it meant in 1789.

I think the paragraphs you quoted are the polarizations of a dilemma we have had since the republic started. Obviously the Constitution has fixed meanings. It is intended to serve as a limitation on government: that used to be taught in law school, when I was there, in a course entitled Constitutional Limitations. And clearly the Constitution is intended to limit not only what Congress can do but, in turn, what the judges can impose on it.

But the framers clearly expected it to constitute, and to be sufficient for, a republic that would go on for a long time. It makes no sense to confine it to only those limitations and only those rights that are specifically spelled out in it.

Let me give an example: the issue of voting, something I know a little bit about. As late as the 1860s, when the Fourteenth Amendment was adopted, there were a lot of limitations on who could vote in this country. Women couldn't vote. People who didn't own property couldn't vote. Slaves couldn't vote. Even when the Fourteenth Amendment was adopted and slaves *could* vote, there were still other limitations.

By the 1950s, we had removed, by constitutional amendment and otherwise, the limitations based on property holdings and the limitations on women voting. So it was not unreasonable for the court in *Baker* v. *Carr* to say that, if sex, race, and property were not relevant limitations on the right to vote, then clearly geography should not be a limitation on the right to vote. Today even conservative scholars would acknowledge that *Baker* v. *Carr* was not a revolutionary break from constitutional law.

We have to read what both the attorney general and Justice Brennan say, and remember both statements when we are trying to decide these awesome cases.

J. CLIFFORD WALLACE, Judge, U.S. Court of Appeals: I suppose the basic question is, How do we, as a people, provide for social change? The focus is always on the courts, for some reason, and perhaps during this next hour we will be able to explore why that is so. When the Constitution established a means of governing the people, it did not give just the courts that responsibility. People have a tendency to look at the courts in a vacuum, without recognizing that the framers, in their wisdom, had in mind an overall process for governing the people.

The essential plan, it seems to me, was to develop a system of democracy that really works. There were some aspects of democracy that worried the framers, so the Constitution, together with the Bill of Rights, sets up certain protections of minority individual rights. But except for those limited areas, the idea, as I understand it, was that the people, through their elected representatives, would provide the voice for social change. Our belief in this basic democratic process governs how we feel about the courts and their role in interpreting the Constitution.

Except in the area of certain individual rights that are protected by the Constitution, the courts should allow the people's elected representatives to decide social change, even though the courts may think, politically or sociologically, that a decision is wrong. It must always be remembered that the courts, in essence, are antidemocratic and can overrule the majority. And when judges, appointed for life, are exercising this very important power, they should be wary of such antidemocratic forays. They should be careful to allow the legislature and the executive to carry out their responsibilities under the Constitution.

Because judicial restraint is based on respect for the other branches, I would align myself with that basic philosophy.

LAURENCE TRIBE, Professor, Harvard Law School: Obviously this is a very large question, to which we are asked to give a brief answer. To focus on where social change should come from, however, is misleading.

For example, the philosophy of Mr. Meese would interpose courts, in the name of the Constitution, as a break upon social change engineered by affirmative action programs. Justice Brennan's perspective would leave society and the political process freer to implement race-conscious programs. It is a dangerous oversimplification to see the issue as one of social change retarded or engineered by the courts.

In answer to the broad question, How should we interpret the Constitution? we should begin with the fact that it is a living legal document. It is a legal document designed to endure and to constitute a political society, but it *is* a legal document. Reading it is radically different from the process of writing one of your own. There are many things I would like to have in an ideal constitution (occasionally I have

134

helped other countries write them) that I can't find in our Constitution.

But trying to read the Constitution according to the specific brain waves and mind states of the authors of the document would, quite paradoxically, be incompatible with their broad original intent. The framers wanted to launch into history a document that would endure and evolve. When they wanted to be very narrow and precise and specific, they knew how. They required that the president be thirty-five instead of "sufficiently mature." In other parts of the Constitution, they spoke more capaciously—about cruel and unusual punishment, about the privileges of national citizenship, about due process of law, about equal protection.

The examples they had in mind when they used those phrases were not legislated in concrete. The convention that ratified the Fourteenth Amendment, for instance, did not ratify the examples that occurred to the authors of that amendment. We know, for example, that those authors were themselves quite satisfied that segregated public education should persist in the face of the Fourteenth Amendment. Yet it would be a radical mistake—and Mr. Meese concedes that it would be a mistake in one of his speeches—to suppose, therefore, that the original intent of the framers of the Fourteenth Amendment somehow precludes *Brown* v. *Board of Education.*

Our task, therefore, is to read and understand the Constitution in light of its context and its structure. We should focus on the intent of the document as a whole and as an objective public fact, but not in a way that resembles the psychoanalysis of the private subjective states of mind of the authors. We are dealing with a document that, when it speaks in generalities, should be respected for that choice.

WALTER BERNS, Professor, Georgetown University: For reasons having to do with the republican principles stated in the Declaration of Independence, it seems to me quite obvious we are bound by the intent of the framers when interpreting the Constitution. The intent of the framers is to be found within that text. We need not psychoanalyze the framers or read their autobiographies. We only have to read the text of the Constitution. And that text is a lot clearer than is sometimes suggested by those who say that it is filled with generalities and that we are, of necessity, free to roam as we please.

For example, in the latter part of his speech at Georgetown, Justice Brennan discusses the death penalty. Not only is he opposed to the death penalty, he is firmly persuaded that it is unconstitutional. He comes to that conclusion not because he cannot read the Constitution. He can read the Constitution at least as well as I can read the Constitution. And when he reads the Constitution, he sees five specific references indicating that capital punishment is absolutely constitutional.

The Fifth Amendment permits capital trials, if they are preceded by "a presentment or indictment of a Grand Jury," and a person's life may be put in jeopardy once, but not twice, for the same offense. Furthermore, a person may be deprived of life with due process of law, but not without due process of law. The Fourteenth Amendment repeats that particular provision. Then, of course, in Article 2, Section 2, the president is empowered to issue reprieves. Here, then, are five specific references in the text of the Constitution making it absolutely clear that the death penalty is not unconstitutional.

Justice Brennan, nevertheless—having talked about the magnificent generalities of the text of the Constitution—comes to the conclusion that the death penalty is unconstitutional. Question: By what right does he do this?

PROFESSOR TRIBE: I will not try to defend the conclusion that the death penalty is unconstitutional. I find that problematic. But I find your reading of the text very difficult. Those provisions indicate that, insofar as death is used, it must be used in accord with various safeguards. Perhaps death will be allowed, perhaps it won't.

The cruel and unusual punishment clause makes that an open question. For example, when you referred to not being put twice in jeopardy of life, the Fifth Amendment actually doesn't just say "life," it says "life or limb." I suppose that means we could hack off people's arms.

A fair reading of that provision might indicate that, as long as we use that form of punishment, we had better limit it to one arm per crime, or whatever. But it doesn't say that we can hack a person's arm off. It leaves that question for the interpretation of the cruel and unusual punishment clause. And members of any court I can imagine would now say that lopping off arms is cruel and unusual punishment.

PROFESSOR BERNS: Would your conclusion be that capital punishment is unconstitutional?

PROFESSOR TRIBE: Probably not. I would be delighted by a constitution that barred capital punishment, but I'm inclined to say that it is not yet cruel and unusual. At any rate, the fact that I differ with Justice Brennan on some points and with Chief Justice Rehnquist on others is not to the point.

136

I agree with you that we must read the text to discern intent, but the question is, How are we to go about reading the text? Are we to read it in light of all conceivable negative implications, or are we to read it as a document capable of growth?

The Ninth Amendment is relevant here. It suggests that in reading the Constitution, one should not be narrow-minded about the enumeration of rights. It says that the enumeration of certain rights shall not be taken to deny the existence of others. That was written against a presupposition of limited government to signal the possibility of limitations upon government.

JUDGE MIKVA: I was struck, Professor Berns, by the way you argued that capital punishment is constitutional, referring to five specific places as if the Constitution were actually ordaining capital punishment. Now, I know you didn't mean that. The Bill of Rights—which was not, as you know, the constituting part of the Constitution but was intended to serve as a source of limitations—is where most of what Justice Jackson called the majestic generalities are to be found. At that point the framers were clearly trying to finesse some disagreements they had, and they also were trying to reassure a lot of doubtful people that they were not creating an omnipotent government that would take away all the rights not specifically spelled out in the first five articles of the Constitution. And I thought about using the death penalty as an example.

PROFESSOR BERNS: It's Brennan's example.

JUDGE MIKVA: Let me give you a harder one, if I may. I think you would agree that Justice Frankfurter had a very deep concern about not leaving the text of the Constitution, and that he certainly didn't wander far afield when it came to interpreting some of these majestic generalities. And yet he found that using a stomach pump on a defendant to get evidence was cruel and unusual punishment, that it shocked the conscience, and therefore, couldn't be done.

I remember clerking in the Supreme Court at the time, and I was shocked at his shock, because he was considered a very conservative justice as far as the Bill of Rights was concerned. And yet this so offended his conscience that he felt that it should be declared unconstitutional.

DR. GOLDWIN: Was it cruel and unusual punishment—or unreasonable search? [Laughter.]

JUDGE MIKVA: It was due process.

JUDGE WALLACE: No, it was not unreasonable search.

JUDGE MIKVA: It was one of the other majestic generalities, and the point is that he was applying contemporary standards, because in 1789 the stomach pump was neither constitutional nor unconstitutional, if I can use your paraphrasing.

PROFESSOR BERNS: Obviously, we would not be here discussing this issue if it were simple—

JUDGE MIKVA: Right.

PROFESSOR BERNS:—and one would have to be a fool to argue that it is simple. But I would like to put a question to the two judges on the panel: To what extent are your difficulties derived from the Fourteenth Amendment cases, which provide the bulk of constitutional litigation now? I mean especially due process and equal protection, those two clauses. The original text of the Constitution, I think, is not so difficult to interpret. The difficulty comes with the Fourteenth Amendment, which seemingly is stated in these generalities.

JUDGE WALLACE: There is no question that a large amount of the work we do involves the Fourteenth Amendment. While I was reading briefs for next week's calendar, I was struck that, left unbridled, lawyers with their fertile minds can find a due process or equal protection argument for almost any issue that comes before the courts.

To some extent, their reasoning has a certain amount of logic to it. If I were sitting back and trying to decide what kind of government I would like to have—if I were a benign dictator instead of a judge—I could subscribe to deciding everything on the basis of due process and equal protection. But one must have a certain amount of judicial humility and recognize that that is not a judge's right. There are certain limitations that we must respect.

But the Fourteenth Amendment is treated by some almost as an open-ended invitation to make a constitutional problem out of every complaint before the courts.

I remember, for instance, the first time I sat on a case that suggested there was a constitutional problem because a school principal had directed certain students to have shorter haircuts. There I was, deciding this great constitutional question. And I wondered if that's really what I had in mind when I became an Article III judge.

PROFESSOR TRIBE: It's too easy to make it look as if the whole problem comes from the majestic generalities of the Fourteenth Amendment. The most lively debate in recent years on the meaning of original intent has been conducted within the Supreme Court over the meaning of the religion clauses of the First Amendment.

In one rather famous case, the Alabama legislature had specified a moment of silence for prayer or meditation, specifically using the word "prayer." The Court divided over whether the establishment clause of the First Amendment (in that case it was being applied to the states through the Fourteenth Amendment) should be construed as preventing the government from deliberately endorsing religion, or whether it should be read much more narrowly, as simply preventing the government from discriminating among religions or setting up an official state church.

Justice O'Connor, writing to concur with the majority, said she thought that the establishment clause should be understood in terms of the general intention of the framers to avoid government endorsement of religion. Justice Rehnquist, dissenting, took the view that, because the wall of separation was not directly in the minds of the framers—he pointed out that Jefferson was in Paris at the time—it would be wrong to read the establishment clause that broadly.

Even without getting to words like due process and equal protection, then, one has to choose between those two approaches. As Justice O'Connor pointed out, there were virtually no public schools when the First Amendment was written, so the issue of prayer in the public schools certainly did not occur to the framers. That fact might lead one, if one took a very narrow view of original intention, to say that official prayer in the public schools is just fine.

If, instead, one says the framers knew that the document would outlast the particular social conditions that gave it birth, and that therefore one has to look beneath the surface to what Justice Rehnquist, in another case, called the "tacit postulates" of the Constitution's provisions, then I think one would agree with Justice O'Connor.

So I think the problem does not occur only in Fourteenth Amendment jurisprudence. It occurs throughout the Constitution.

JUDGE WALLACE: That's probably right, Professor Tribe, but how we approach the problem will largely determine the outcome. For example, in a Nebraska case in which a minister was paid to offer a prayer before the legislature, Chief Justice Burger, in his opinion, went back in history, identified the circumstances as they existed at the time of the writing of the Constitution, and applied that historical interpretation. He took the position that we must look to the framers' intent in the sense not only of what they did at the time of the adoption of the Constitution, but also of what was going on at that particular time.

What happened in the past was more carefully examined in that case, perhaps, than in other cases.

JUDGE MIKVA: To answer Professor Berns's question, from what I see both within my circuit and in the other circuits, we probably get more criminal litigation from the Fourth Amendment than from the Fourteenth. There the courts have struggled with "unreasonable search and seizure" and other phrases that perhaps aren't quite as majestic as some others.

PROFESSOR BERNS: Of necessity the courts will struggle with those.

JUDGE MIKVA: And the Congress has struggled with them.

PROFESSOR BERNS: No one argues about that.

JUDGE MIKVA: There is an interplay here, because technology affects our understanding of those words. For instance, the first wiretapping cases before the courts were very difficult. How do you fit wiretapping into the concepts of a warrant and a search of places and things and people?

JUDGE WALLACE: Justice Black had trouble with the wiretaps.

JUDGE MIKVA: Yes, he did. And Congress has had trouble with them. Just recently Congress made another assault on the exclusionary rule, which comes out of the Fourth Amendment.

DR. GOLDWIN: Could you please explain the exclusionary rule?

JUDGE MIKVA: The exclusionary rule says that courts will not consider as evidence material obtained in violation of the Fourth Amendment. It therefore frequently causes a criminal defendant to go free, because the police cannot prove their case without such evidence.

DR. GOLDWIN: Professor Berns spoke of the difficulties of interpreting the Fourteenth Amendment, and Professor Tribe argued that we should consider instead cases coming from the First Amendment. Finally, Judge Mikva spoke of the complications that come from the Fourth Amendment's prohibition of unreasonable search and seizure.

But still, aren't they all related to the Fourteenth Amendment and a big change in the way the Constitution is read? Don't many of the difficulties in interpreting it now come from the Court's decision that the Fourteenth Amendment makes the First Amendment, the Fourth Amendment, and others applicable to the states, whereas they were clearly written, and were always understood, to apply only to the federal government?

Now there is the complication of having to decide, for instance, the meaning of the establishment clause—that there shall not be an establishment of religion—as it applies to the states, whereas previously, it was always understood to apply only to the federal government. This surely makes it much more difficult to interpret the Constitution.

PROFESSOR TRIBE: It does increase the volume of cases in which such issues arise. And the attorney general of the United States a while ago suggested in a speech in London that perhaps the incorporation of the Bill of Rights—its application against the states—should be reconsidered. But he has since reconsidered and appears to have joined nearly a universal consensus that, as George Will noted, if we were to reconsider incorporation, there would be extraordinary chaos. Anyone who wants to undo that would not be fit to sit on a federal court, according to Will. Whether one agrees with that or not, it is misleading to suppose that the problem is seriously accentuated in a qualitative way by the Fourteenth Amendment.

I would like to go back to Judge Wallace's example of the Nebraska chaplain case, in which the state legislature, using public funds, hired a chaplain to introduce the legislative session with a prayer. Justice Stevens dissented from the Court's decision upholding this practice, and he pointed out the serious dangers involved in picking and choosing among religions. He maintained that one is not likely to find followers of Mary Baker Eddy or Sun Myung Moon leading many of these state legislative prayers.

But Chief Justice Burger for the majority focused, as Judge Wallace noted, on the history. He said that at the time the First Amendment was written, prayers of this kind were common and therefore it follows—perhaps not inexorably but presumptively—that the Constitution doesn't condemn them. Judge Wallace, are you saying that approach is congenial to you?

JUDGE WALLACE: No, I was pointing that out as one approach the Supreme Court has taken—

PROFESSOR TRIBE: From time to time. But if it took that approach very often, look what would happen. If it took that approach to the Fourteenth Amendment, for instance, what would follow? Because segregated public schools were common when the Fourteenth Amendment was written and ratified, and were not then thought to be unconstitutional, it would follow that it was somehow too radical for the Court in *Brown* v. *Board of Education* to have undone that.

JUDGE WALLACE: It's interesting, Professor Tribe, that every time I've been in one of these discussions with people who adhere to the "living constitution" theory, *Brown* v. *Board of Education* is always the example.

JUDGE MIKVA: I didn't cite *Brown* v. *Board*—

JUDGE WALLACE: You will. [Laughter.]

JUDGE MIKVA:—but then I don't adhere to the "living constitution." I cited *Baker* v. *Carr.*

JUDGE WALLACE: But who's going to decide what the current "living constitution" dictates? That is, if we refuse to use the founders' game plan because it's two centuries old, and if today's problems require a "living constitution"—who will decide what that constitution compels? The decision will be made by nine people who sit on the Supreme Court in Washington, D.C.

The assumption is that a "living constitution" is beneficial for us, and that the Court will always make the right decisions when they make this constitution live and change. How can we guarantee that? It seems to me that those who decry the substantive due process decisions of the 1930s, when President Roosevelt's programs were being overturned by *that* period's "living constitution," which was a "conservative" judicial activism of that time, must also take a dim view of subsequent judicial activism of a "liberal" type.

If the character of the "living constitution" depends upon who the nine justices are, then we have to say, "Okay, if the nine happen to belong to the Ku Klux Klan, I'll still allow them to make the 'living constitution' alive for me." I'm not ready to accept that. If the founders took such pains to say the Constitution can be changed only by the formal process of amendment, then it's difficult for me to accept amendment by sociological surveys.

JUDGE MIKVA: Judge Wallace, you point out exactly how difficult these choices are, because we tend to try to resolve them by hurling slogans at each other. Now, I didn't hear Professor Tribe use the term "living constitution." I don't know whether he likes that idea or not. I don't particularly like it, because it suggests that there is no restraint at all, just going from judge to judge, and from year to year.

DR. GOLDWIN: Professor Tribe urged us to remember that the Constitution is a "living legal document."

JUDGE MIKVA: "Legal document," he said.

DR. GOLDWIN: Is that different from a constitution?

JUDGE MIKVA: It's different from the notion that you can just pick and choose and say, "I like this. I don't like that. Therefore, I'll go with this and not go with that, and here's a new idea that nobody thought of. I'll put that in." Those are the connotations of the words "living constitution."

The fact is, these choices are very hard, and yet Judge Wallace suggests that there is somehow a judge machine, into which we put the facts, and then the constitutional provision, and out comes a decision. He knows better than that. He knows that these are struggles.

I happen to agree both with *Brown* v. *Board, and* with the Chief Justice in the chaplain case. And I agree with the Chief Justice, not only because of the history of the meaning of that clause—because there was a chaplain praying over the Congress that adopted that amendment—but also because even today, if we go into the House of Representatives or the Senate of the United States, we find a chaplain praying for the souls of those members. And those prayers are needed. [Laughter.]

JUDGE MIKVA: There's a paid marshal saying "God save the United States and this honorable court" every day when we start to sit. The point I make is that there were tremendous changes in the practice of school segregation between 1865 and 1954, when *Brown* v. *Board* was decided. There was a topographical change in our culture, in our institutions, and in voting habits.

But there hasn't been that kind of sea change in the way we treat religion in our political institutions. So I think both decisions are defensible.

PROFESSOR TRIBE: Could I disagree with that? Although I almost never find myself in disagreement with you.

The reason I use *Brown* v. *Board of Education* as an example is that it illustrates in a powerful way, applicable in other areas, that we are not taking a sociological poll or looking at changing demographics when we look at this as a legal document. That is, I think we have to take seriously that those who wrote and ratified the Fourteenth Amendment used the words "equal protection of the laws." We have to make a conscientious effort to give meaning to that concept, equal protection.

In *Plessy* v. *Ferguson*, the case dealing with separate but equal facilities, the Court, I think, made a fundamental mistake. It's not just that it was an old decision. The Court concluded that the separation of blacks and whites—despite the obvious message it sent to black people that they were inferior—constituted equal protection of the laws. That is, there is equal protection as long as the facilities are physically equal.

Then a more recent court took the position, I think correctly, that separation is inherently unequal, in any setting where the understandable meaning of the separation is inequality. That interpretation did not result from a demographic change, although that might help explain why later judges were more sensitive to this insight. But I do not think that judges in that case amended the Constitution to keep pace with the times. That would be wrong—we have a specific procedure for amending the Constitution.

Judicial humility needs to be encouraged, but it is not encouraged by the illusion that some *method* can make outcomes independent of who the nine justices are. All of us sitting around this table *know* that the questions are hard and that the answers are not automatic.

No method of interpreting a document as complex as this, with as subtle a history as it has, will eliminate our dependence on who the justices are. I'm afraid that the so-called jurisprudence of original intention, far from encouraging humility, will in fact encourage arrogance under a cloak of humility, as Justice Brennan suggested in his speech. It will permit people to say, "I'm just applying what I scientifically discover the intent of the framers to be," when, in fact, there will always be difficult choices along the way. We should admit we make choices, and then we should explain, in terms of the text and the structure, how we get to the conclusion that we think is correct.

DR. GOLDWIN: Let me pose a question by quoting one sentence from Justice Brennan: "Judicial power resides," he says, "in the power to give meaning to the Constitution."

Now, another way of saying something *like* that would be, "Judicial power resides in the power to *ascertain* the meaning of the Constitution." Is there a fundamental difference of approach in saying "give meaning" to the Constitution and in saying "ascertain the meaning" of the Constitution?

PROFESSOR BERNS: Of course there's a fundamental difference. The implication of Justice Brennan's statement is that the Constitution means absolutely nothing until I, William J. Brennan, Jr., say what it means.

JUDGE MIKVA: But a reading of the whole speech shows clearly that that is not the context in which that line was used. He went on to say very clearly, "I realize that we are not final because we are infallible."

PROFESSOR BERNS: That's Justice Robert Jackson.

JUDGE MIKVA: Well, he quoted Jackson, and he quoted it in a long paragraph, in which he made it clear that he was aware that these are awesome decisions and that an antidemocratic or a nondemocratic institution is making these decisions. So I don't think you find the kind of arrogance or disdain for the written words that the line taken out of context suggests.

PROFESSOR BERNS: Who can more rightly be accused of being arrogant? Someone who reads those five provisions in the Constitution having to do with the death penalty and then insouciantly says it is unconstitutional? Or someone who does his best to understand the text, and then comes to a conclusion? Who can be more rightly accused of being arrogant?

PROFESSOR TRIBE: We could become very *ad hominem* about who's arrogant and who isn't, but that's not what I meant to do.

PROFESSOR BERNS: The term is Justice Brennan's.

PROFESSOR TRIBE: But the term is applied to a method, and not to a person. I'm really not talking about who's arrogant and who's humble. I'm talking about avoiding methods of interpretation that invite us into various pretenses.

There is a difference between ascertaining meaning and pouring meaning in as though into an empty vessel. I couldn't defend the latter, but I honestly don't believe that Justice Brennan or anyone else on the Court thinks he's engaged in such behavior.

DR. GOLDWIN: Then let me give you one other sentence from Justice Brennan, which is a little different: "The ultimate question must be, What do the words of the text mean in our time?" Now that means you have to look at the words, right? But do you see a significant difference in that formulation?

PROFESSOR BERNS: Yes. Let me say something that I wanted to say a moment ago, and it's relevant here, too.

Justice Brennan uses the phrase "for a time that's dead and gone," in his Georgetown speech. And in your initial presentation, Judge Mikva, you referred to the extent to which voting habits have changed, and so the Constitution has to be changed, and so on. I want to say to Judge Mikva that he exaggerates the extent to which the Constitution is out of date.

In fact, not a word in the Constitution had to be changed to allow women to vote, to allow blacks to vote, to allow women to hold office, to allow women to serve on your court, or to allow women to serve on the Supreme Court of the United States or as vice president or president of the United States. *Not one word* had to be changed.

JUDGE MIKVA: Well, that gets back to the question of what you call constitutional. Section 4 of Article I specifically says that "times, places and manner of holding elections for Senators and Representatives shall be prescribed in each state by the legislature thereof." And the legislatures thereof, in all those states, had rules against voting by nonproperty owners, women, and the young. The Constitution changed all that by saying that no one shall be denied the right to vote. So technically you are correct. We didn't change the words of Section 4, Article I.

We also didn't change the words of the article which says that slaves will be sent back to the state from whence they came, when we passed the Fourteenth Amendment.

PROFESSOR BERNS: But the Constitution didn't use the word "slaves." That is further evidence that the Constitution was not written as an eighteenth century document to survive for a few decades into the nineteenth.

JUDGE MIKVA: In that we are in total agreement.

PROFESSOR BERNS: And it had to be changed very little to make it possible for us to live happily and uniquely free among all the countries of the world in the twentieth century.

JUDGE MIKVA: We can agree that it is a tribute, that during the past 200 years we have had only twenty-six occasions to go back and amend the Constitution with ten amendments immediately following the framing of the Constitution.

DR. GOLDWIN: And two of the twenty-six amendments cancelled each other. But I have to interrupt at this moment of unique agreement between Professor Berns and Judge Mikva to move on to the question and answer session. May I have the first question please?

FRED QUINN, U.S. Information Agency: What advice do our panelists have for constitution–writers in Africa, Europe, Latin America, and Asia who are struggling with the questions of writing or revising constitutions?

JUDGE MIKVA: I just made a speech on this to the proposed constitution writers in Brazil. I hope—and I am not very confident this hope will be fulfilled—that they take the nonspecificity of our Constitution as their model. I worry deeply that they are putting everything into their Constitution, including the kitchen sink. They are trying to guarantee all kinds of economic rights, like the right to a job, the right to a home, and the right to food—and while I am all for those rights, they can't be guaranteed in any of those countries. So the constitution will be a dead letter before the ink is even dry on the document.

I wish instead they would incorporate some of those majestic

147

generalities that we are arguing about. Then they would have a document that would survive.

PROFESSOR TRIBE: Sometimes easier said than done, though. When I helped the Marshall Islands to write a constitution I started exactly with Judge Mikva's preference: I wanted majestic generalities. But they pointed out that they lived in far-flung islands and didn't trust each other to legislate, so they wanted to pin it all down. They ended up with a very detailed, 85-page document, which guaranteed, among other things, protection against newsroom searches. When we help other countries to write constitutions, we have to recognize that we cannot necessarily export our capacity to be brief.

PROFESSOR BERNS: I was in Brazil last year, too, talking about the constitution. I ran into the same thing that Judge Mikva was talking about and offered the same sort of advice. I would add one thing, however. It is important for these countries to realize that they cannot achieve constitutional government by relying on judicial review alone.

Jurists from around the world look to the Constitution of the United States and its happy bicentennial existence and attribute that to the fact that rights have been secured by the Supreme Court. In fact, of course, the first time the Supreme Court enforced a First Amendment right against the Congress of the United States was in 1965. The first time it enforced a religious provision against Congress was in 1971. We tend to forget that.

As Madison said in *Federalist* No. 51, we have civil and religious rights in this country because of the peculiar structure of our Constitution. We could not simply rely on judges. That is, with respect to the federal government, the states are a different proposition altogether. That is an important piece of advice to give to people around the world.

JUDGE WALLACE: Having worked with judiciaries in fourteen Asian countries on behalf of the Asia Foundation, I have concluded that they must learn more than just the words. Our document tells how we as a people are constituted. It has survived because of something more than the document and the words. Other countries have tried copying our Constitution and have not succeeded as we have. And if I have any message for those who are struggling with a constitution, it is to identify what they are trying to accomplish for their people. That perhaps is more important than the precise words that are written.

PROFESSOR BERNS: May I add one other thing, Mr. Quinn—and this, I think, should be said in Brazil, too. We get smug about the brevity of the Constitution and its glittering generalities. We must always remember that when that Constitution was written there were thirteen states with written constitutions that went into great detail with respect to a whole body of material. Under a federal system that was possible, and that is one reason why our Constitution was so brief.

DR. GOLDWIN: As I understand these answers, we should advise other countries to have a federal union with a short federal constitution—and then they will have all the troubles interpreting their constitution that we have been having with ours.

JUDGE MIKVA: Maybe some countries aren't ready for a constitution. That is the position taken by several Israeli scholars—that the country is just not ready to write and commit itself to a formal constitution, because they have not achieved the homogeneity that we had in this country. They will have to struggle some more before they reach that point. And I think Judge Wallace is right, that just putting something down on a piece of paper and waving it around will not make one country out of a lot of warring tribes.

PROFESSOR TRIBE: When you say "not ready," of course the United Kingdom, which has quite an old history, still doesn't have a written constitution, and doesn't feel it needs one.

JUDGE MIKVA: They may have passed the point of any dispute.

PROFESSOR TRIBE: But if one is needed, it probably must be made judicially enforceable. South Africa and the Soviet Union have wonderful-sounding phrases in their constitutions, but they are not worth the paper they are written on, largely because, if judges try to enforce them, they can be removed or relocated—or worse.

ALFRED MOLLINS, U.S. Department of Justice: I've had to endure Judge Mikva's questions in the courtroom many times, and the chance to return the favor may never occur again, so I thought I would jump in. [Laughter.]

Judge Mikva, you and Professor Tribe have responded to these questions largely by referring to generalities in the Constitution and by suggesting that they need interpretation and construction. But that doesn't seem to me a full answer, because the generalities themselves do have limits. There are fixed subject areas in which the Constitution intends to have the Court work.

Let me pose as the counter, say, to *Brown* v. *Board of Education* another example, the abortion decision. As far as I can see, there was not even a magnificent generality within which the Court could locate its decision. The Court talks about penumbras, about shadows, about privacy rights—although the word privacy never does occur in the Constitution. Does that show contempt on the part of the majority of the Court for any limitation whatsoever?

JUDGE MIKVA: If the question is directed to me, let me say that there are several phrases in the Constitution that talk about inferior courts, and I am a judge on one of those inferior courts. When the Supreme Court hands down a decision that covers a subject, it is the law of the land, as far as I am concerned. Whatever freedom all of you have to criticize a decision of the Supreme Court of the United States specifically, as an inferior judge on a subordinate court I accept it and try to apply it in future cases.

There are generalities involved, though, in the general abortion area. We are talking about the general question of due process of law. Part of your concern, I assume, deals with the Court's suggestion in *Roe* v. *Wade* that there is a right to privacy, when, as you correctly note, the Constitution does not mention any right to privacy. If I were one of the bosses instead of one of the inferiors, maybe I would not have parsed out that situation the way the Court did in *Roe* v. *Wade*. Maybe I would have waited, because I believe a lot in the topography in which a Supreme Court decision comes down. Justice Brennan talked about that when he referred to the legitimacy of the decision. It troubles me a great deal that *Roe* v. *Wade* has continued to generate so much hostility to the Court and to the judicial review function. During my last year in the Congress of the United States, we spent more time debating abortion, measured by pages of the *Congressional Record*, than any other decision—and that was some fifteen years after *Roe* v. *Wade* came down. That disturbs me a great deal. Maybe it would have been better if the Court had waited on *Roe* v. *Wade*. Progress was being made at the political levels: some states were changing their abortion laws—New York, for instance. And I still have a picture somewhere of Governor Reagan signing a very extensive liberalization of the California abortion law with great gusto and saying that it would get the abortions out of the streets and alleys and into the doctors' offices where they belong. I gather he's had a change of view since then.

But, again, the academicians here can debate whether it would

150

have been better for the Court to have stayed its hand. Judge Wallace and I remember our position.

DR. GOLDWIN: But is that your primary concern, that the timing was wrong?

JUDGE MIKVA: A lot can be said about the legitimacy of a case in terms of its timing. Let me give you an example, and again, I would use Justice Frankfurter. *Brown* v. *Board* was argued the first time while I was clerking there, in 1951–1952. And we invited Justice Frankfurter down one day for lunch. A clerk asked: "Mr. Justice, why isn't *Brown* v. *Board of Education* coming down this year—it's already been argued and circulated?" And he looked at us, and said: "You wouldn't want us to come down with a decision like that in an election year, would you?"

Well, we were horrified. The notion that the national elections were influencing when the Supreme Court of the United States would come down with cases was incredible to a group of fresh young law students. And yet it was 1952. If it had been put out then, as Justice Frankfurter said, it would probably have been chewed up by the two candidates. Governor Stevenson probably would have supported the decision, maybe General Eisenhower would have opposed it. Then what would have happened in Little Rock several years later when the federal government was called upon to enforce that decree?

In retrospect, given the difficulty we have had digesting the fruits of *Brown* v. *Board of Education*, maybe Justice Frankfurter had more correctness on his side than I thought at the time.

PROFESSOR BERNS: I don't think there is any quarrel about considering the timing. I think Professor Goldwin, when he asked that question, had in mind an additional reason, and perhaps even a more important reason, why in our judgment the Court was wrong to do what it did when it decided *Roe* v. *Wade*.

When the Court does that sort of thing—let me start with my conclusion—it gets into politics. It creates a right, in this particular case a right to privacy, which it then defines. To speak of a right is to describe an area exempt from political power. That's what a right means: the political processes may not govern here, may not enter. This is an area that is exempt from politics.

Before one does that sort of thing, especially before one talks about a fundamental right, one ought to be doggone certain that there is some agreement that it is in fact a fundamental right. At the beginning of this country we instituted a government, under the prescriptions of the Declaration of Independence, in order to secure certain rights. We agreed about those rights.

But if the Declaration of Independence had said, "We hold these truths to be self-evident, that all men are created equal, that they are endowed by their Creator with certain unalienable rights, that among these are life, liberty, and *sodomy,*" for example—I don't think we could have had a United States of America. I don't think we could have constituted a government on the basis of *those* rights, whether the Supreme Court of the United States described them as fundamental rights or not. That was the problem with the Court in *Roe.*

Now, Mr. Tribe was counsel in the sodomy case, so he is going to have something to say about it, I'm sure.

PROFESSOR TRIBE: Yes, I think you're right. [Laughter.]

It seems to me that it misstates the question to ask whether the catalog of fundamental rights includes sodomy, abortion, and the like. The relevant right is the right to live under a system of limited government in which, when government intrudes into the most personal spheres of life, the Court will demand of the government a more particularized justification than some states have sometimes given.

That's a principle that I think is ingrained tacitly in the entire Constitution, and certainly in the Bill of Rights and in the Ninth Amendment. Without that principle, the Court's decisions protecting people's rights to decide whether to have children and how to bring them up, decisions in the 1920s about the right to send our children to a private school—all of those decisions would be wiped away.

What is excruciatingly difficult about the abortion case is not whether the word "liberty"—which, after all, is in the Fourteenth Amendment—is or is not capacious enough to encompass a woman's control over her own reproductive capacity. What makes the case excruciatingly and tragically difficult is the compelling character of the countervailing interest in protecting the life of the fetus. And that's why that case is so extraordinarily difficult from any perspective. Anything the Court would have done could easily have been claimed by some to have violated someone's rights—the rights of the woman or the rights of the unborn.

By contrast, the Court by a five-to-four vote said the states may do essentially what they want and outlaw private consenting noncommercial sexual acts. But eventually this country will see that that issue is not as difficult as the abortion issue, because there isn't the same kind of countervailing interest in protecting another being.

However we come out in any of these cases, unless we read the

Constitution partly in terms of its tacit postulates, we are lost. Justice Rehnquist does that when it comes to states' rights. In an opinion joined by Chief Justice Burger, he pointed out that the tacit postulates of the constitutional plan are, in his words, "as much ingrained in the fabric of the document as are its express provisions."

If one didn't believe that, then the very language of the Tenth Amendment—that powers delegated to the national government are not reserved to the states—would empower Congress to obliterate state governments. The method of reading the Constitution recognizing tacit rights for states ought also to be applied in a way that recognizes tacit rights for families and for individuals, although in some cases, when there are countervailing claims of right, one has an extraordinarily tragic and difficult choice.

JUDGE WALLACE: Didn't it make for a strange situation, though, when Justice Douglas talked about these penumbra of rights, as if we could see some sort of shadow coming out, not really knowing where it is, or where it ends.

PROFESSOR TRIBE: "The Shadow knows." [Laughter.]

JUDGE WALLACE: Yes, "The Shadow knows." You are showing your age, by the way. [Laughter.]

I agree with Judge Mikva that an inferior court judge takes what comes down from the Supreme Court. But when the Court uses the penumbra approach, and finds all these rights that aren't spelled out but somehow emanate from the Constitution, an ambiguity is created. Then, after they have created the ambiguity, they try to define the ambiguity and to develop rights out of the ambiguity. That isn't really the same as finding a right that is spelled out in the Constitution.

DR. GOLDWIN: Gentlemen, I think we have to go on to the next question.

PROFESSOR BERNS: We are not finished with this one, by any means.

JUDGE MIKVA: I think we'll get back to it.

JIM UNGAR, National Forensics Institute: At some risk, I would like to return to what I think was the original topic for this panel, as indicated by the title. My suspicion is that the emphasis falls on the word

"How," and I was wondering if each member of the panel could tell us succinctly what he sees as the legitimate resources to turn to in interpreting the Constitution.

Obviously we have the text. We have what Professor Tribe has referred to, and what the old and new chief justices talked about, the postulates ingrained in the text, as well. But are there other legitimate sources of constitutional interpretation?

PROFESSOR BERNS: Reference has been made to *Baker* v. *Carr* a couple of times. I will now refer to one of its progeny, *Gray* v. *Sanders,* and then *Reynolds* v. *Sims,* where the statement was repeated. These cases have to do with legislative reapportionment, and *Reynolds* v. *Sims* specifically has to do with the question of whether the rule of "one man, one equally weighted vote," applies to the second house of state legislatures. That's the question: How does one interpret the Constitution of the United States to answer that particular question, which came to the Court first in 1963.

Justice Douglas in *Gray* v. *Sanders* sought guidance from the course of American political thought, extending from the Declaration of Independence to Lincoln's Gettysburg Address, and he came to a conclusion that, I think, history does not sustain. Had he, instead, looked at the *Records of the Federal Convention* or *The Federalist* about representation, and their references to the necessity to impose some republican limits on the diseases of republican government, had he looked at Thomas Jefferson, who was after all the principal author of the Declaration of Independence, had he looked at Jefferson's *Notes on the State of Virginia* with respect to this question of representation, he would have found in Query No. 13, "The purpose of establishing different houses of legislation is to introduce the influence of different interests or different principles."

I maintain that if one looks to the text and to those documents that amplify the text, that indicate what the text might have meant to the men who wrote it, such as Jefferson's writings, *The Federalist,* and so forth, one can see that the Court was simply wrong in *Reynolds* v. *Sims*—simply wrong.

JUDGE MIKVA: I certainly would not disagree with Professor Berns on constitutional history, but Justice Douglas made a few other points, particularly with respect to the establishment of the Senate at the federal level. The composition of the U.S. Senate was quite controversial, and at least partly a political compromise designed to offset concern by the little states that the big states might swallow them up.

Professor Berns is not wrong, but Justice Douglas referred to some of those other facts as well.

In addition—and this is where Professor Berns and I may disagree—I sense that he finds it illegitimate for the Court to have looked at anything beyond the founding documents. I think that's wrong. One is entitled to look—one must look—at what has happened in this country in the approximately two hundred years since the founding.

PROFESSOR BERNS: And what do you find, Judge Mikva? Let's look at *Lucas* v. *44th General Assembly of Colorado*, the case decided the same day as *Reynolds* v. *Sims*. Colorado had put a constitutional plan to the people of the state, and a statewide majority—indeed, a majority in every single county in the state—endorsed the principle that the second house of that state legislature could be based on a principle other than one man, one vote. Now, what do we look at?

JUDGE MIKVA: You remind me of what Justice Frankfurter said when we asked him about *Colegrove* v. *Green*, in the days when the Supreme Court was saying it would not get involved in the political thicket of reapportionment. Two of us who were from Illinois said: "But, Justice Frankfurter, what do you expect those of us who are being underrepresented in the state of Illinois to do about this problem?" He said, "Go back there and straighten it out with your politicians."

Well, I served ten years in the Illinois General Assembly, and I can assure you that politicians do not give up political power just because it's the right thing to do. [Laughter.]

And majorities don't give rights to minorities because it's the right thing to do. The whole concept of rights suggests that we are dealing with something that should not be put to a majoritarian test. Obviously the state of Colorado, and maybe even originally the state of Illinois, had ratified constitutions that provided for the second house to be selected on something other than population. But if the sole source of authority, Professor Berns, is what the majority wants, then get rid of the whole Bill of Rights.

PROFESSOR BERNS: That's not my argument.

JUDGE MIKVA: Of course it is. I, on the other hand, referred to what had happened over time. We decided that sex, race, age, and property were no longer meaningful bases for distinguishing among voters and that those bases for distinctions that had been legitimate when the Constitution and the Fourteenth Amendment were adopted should no longer be allowed.

PROFESSOR BERNS: You judges decided that. The people of Colorado did not decide that.

JUDGE MIKVA: No, several of those were put into the Constitution, such as the right of women to enjoy suffrage, the abolition of slavery in the Thirteenth Amendment, and the poll tax amendment. But the Court is entitled to look at history and say that if all these other factors are no longer relevant distinctions, then geography isn't either. You know, when Senator Dirksen and I were debating reapportionment once, he defended geographical distinctions to protect interest groups. I said, "Senator Dirksen, you know, other countries have used interest groups as a basis of representation, and it's perfectly legitimate. The Soviet Union, for instance, uses interest groups—the Soviets are elected from the factories and the farms and the collectives." He grew very silent, and at the end of the program he turned to me and said, "Nobody ever called me a Communist before." [Laughter.]

I'm not calling you a Communist, but the history of this country suggests that geography, not interest groups, determined representation in the general house.

PROFESSOR TRIBE: This is a good example, though, of what really frightens me about the alleged jurisprudence of original intent. This is a subject which we have now tried to cover in perhaps three minutes. I sometimes spend three months on it in a constitutional law course.

JUDGE MIKVA: Professor Berns and I have spent twenty years going back and forth on it.

PROFESSOR TRIBE: But the idea that there exists a method at the conclusion of which one can say, "The Court was simply wrong," with the degree of certitude that you purport to have—that scares me. These are genuinely difficult, debatable issues. Any method that makes the electorate think of judges as robots or history machines—so that when the input is plugged in a certainly correct answer comes out—that method does not conduce to judicial humility. That method makes the courts least accountable in a democracy.

JUDGE WALLACE: Let me respond, as one of those who has been struggling for the past sixteen years to explain how we go about deciding constitutional questions.

In my judgment, every person should start with the text itself. I

156

don't think any judge could or would justifiably start without going to it. The text itself does not give every possible answer. There are some great overarching principles that are discussed within the Constitution. After looking at the text, a person can look at those norms that are clearly expressed within the Constitution.

For example, the structure of the Constitution establishes, very clearly, ways of protecting liberty. One is federalism: it divided the power between the states on the one side and the federal government on the other, a separation of powers. There was a second separation of powers within the federal government, among the three branches.

Those structures tell us a lot about how to approach a given interpretation of the Constitution. Those structures identify the role of the court and the role of the Congress, as the elected representatives of the people.

Now, after leaving the structure, a lot of people—and I happen to be one of them—believe in looking to the framers' intent. And that can be understood from the debates at the convention and the debates on adoption. I don't think the principles discussed therein are dead at all, just because they happen to be two hundred years old.

The framers laid down these basic principles and said: These will govern. They didn't say these principles will govern with a sunset clause of twenty years; they said simply that these principles will govern. They had in mind that these principles, as interpreted, would last through the history of the Republic. And my judgment is, that's fair.

This doesn't mean, as properly suggested by Professor Tribe, that we just plug in the facts and automatically an answer comes out. Of course we apply discretion. But there's a difference between starting with these basic norms of the Constitution to make a decision and simply deciding what an individual judge believes is good for society today.

PROFESSOR TRIBE: I certainly agree with that, but look at your sentence: the framers decided *these principles* shall govern. Principles, not a laundry list of examples. And then we can debate what the underlying principles are. Do they include a general principle of limited government? I believe they do. Do they include the general principle of checks and balances? I believe they do.

Those principles are alive and well today because we understand them at a level of generality as relevant today as earlier, precisely because we do not reduce them to a rather trivial set of illustrations frozen in history.

PROFESSOR BERNS: Does the principle of separation of powers embodied in the Constitution include the principle that the two houses can be based on different concepts of representation?

PROFESSOR TRIBE: Certainly the two houses of the U.S. Congress can, but that is because of the great compromise that created the Senate. It is not at all clear that a similar principle is applicable to state legislatures and local government.

PROFESSOR BERNS: I will say merely I see nothing in the Constitution of the United States that prohibits the states from following the sage advice of the founders with respect to the federal principle.

WARREN CIKINS, the Brookings Institution: I speak as a political scientist, not as a lawyer. I sense a role reversal as I review the history of our country in the treatment of this question. The same people who looked to Congress and the president during the New Deal to effectuate social and economic change in opposition to the courts, are now looking to the courts for such change, in opposition to the legislature or other aspects of our society. In dealing with this question, is there not at least some ingredient of "Whose ox is gored?"

PROFESSOR TRIBE: It's the party whose ox is gored that will develop philosophical grounds for complaint. But the situations are not really symmetrical. That is, the division now is not really between those who want to use the courts as their engine of social change and those who do not. No one is suggesting, for instance, that a redistribution of income ought to be achieved through the courts. It is suggested, however, that when that redistribution is legislatively achieved, the courts ought to stay their hand. That follows from the great constitutional revolution of 1937, when courts began to recognize a larger role for government and the public sector in the regulation of the economy.

Indeed there are people who believe that the courts went too far and that rights of personal property and economic liberty were sacrificed unduly. But that is quite separate from the question of whether or not the preservation of a boundary between the public and the private sphere—which goes to the very core of our system of government—is the appropriate mission of the courts.

One can make fun of words like "penumbras," but, after all, the Ninth Amendment does say there are rights that are not enumerated. And both the people who loved the New Deal and those who opposed it can agree that certain principles of limitation on government power are ingrained in the entire constitutional structure.

JUDGE WALLACE: Mr. Cikins makes a good point. If a principle for interpreting the Constitution varies depending on whose ox is gored, then it's not a principle worthy of being adopted in constitutional interpretation. If a person today believes in social engineering by the courts, he should have believed in similar social engineering in the 1930s.

But a jurisprudence of judicial restraint would be opposed to social engineering no matter who the judge–engineer was. That is, a true jurisprudence of judicial restraint does not have any party affiliation; it is a neutral principle. And it would apply no matter what kind of social engineering was attempted or who tried to do it.

JUDGE MIKVA: Most cases that have given rise to complaints that the Supreme Court has been too activist, where they get involved with government at all, have to do with electoral rights, such as the reapportionment cases. They are difficult and still controversial. But most of the other cases critics complain about are in the area of criminal law and the impact of government on an individual person, as distinguished from what we used to call the substantive due-process cases of the New Deal, which had to do with limits on government's power to affect society as a whole. Those cases dealt, for instance, with the limitation on the government's right to get involved in labor relations and in setting wage-and-hour laws that would affect everybody.

Obviously people have different views on some of those questions, but they are not simply a matter of whose ox is being gored. The hardest case for me, as you may have gathered from a previous question, is the abortion case. I worry about the fact that there are no words like "privacy" and "penumbra" in the Constitution. But the word "children" isn't in the Constitution either. And in my political days, when people used to harass me for my views on the issue of abortion and what the Court had done, I would say, "Well, suppose Congress were to pass a law saying that nobody may have more than two children. That's not an unreasonable proposition. A lot of countries in the world have exactly that kind of law. Are you sure that you wouldn't want the courts to sustain your individual right to have more than two children, even though the word "children" is never mentioned in the Fifth Amendment, the Fourteenth Amendment, or any place else in the Constitution of the United States?"

PROFESSOR TRIBE: And if the courts did that, would we accuse them of social engineering, or would we say that they were putting limits on social engineering, on meddling with the most intimate aspects of the human fabric? I don't advocate social engineering through the courts; I advocate reading the Constitution. But I think the Constitution gives us some answers, though they are not automatic ones, to questions of just this kind.

VICTORIA SHUCK, National Municipal League: In the 1960s, the National Municipal League was the instrument of constitutional change in the states and wrote a model state constitution that was supposed to be patterned on the federal Constitution, with, for example, generalities rather than a laundry list of civil rights.

A short time ago, *The New York Times* noted a new mood among the states with regard to constitutional change, quite different from the one originally mentioned here, namely, a clinging to the status quo.

This suggests that maybe there is a new method of writing constitutions in the United States; perhaps the laundry list is not so bad, because at present some of the states, at any rate, are serving as the avant garde for constitutional change with respect to rights. The new constitution of the District of Columbia is an example of that. What advice would you give the writers of the model constitution today with respect to state constitutions?

DR. GOLDWIN: Do you have anything to say, Mr. Berns, on the District of Columbia constitution as a model?

PROFESSOR BERNS: No. [Laughter.]

JUDGE MIKVA: I have something to say about specific state constitutions. I lived and served under one when I was in the state legislature of Illinois. We discussed everything in our state constitution of 1848, from "constant ferrymen" to the rights of certain groups to be exempt from jury duty to you name it.

Those specific, detailed constitutions tend to become outdated very quickly. I understand the difficulties that Professor Berns and Professor Tribe talked about in asking other countries not to spell out everything—that it is easier advice to give than to take. But it seems to me, given our state history and our country's history, that state constitutions are better off doing their thing in general terms, rather than trying to anticipate every contingency in the next hundred years.

PROFESSOR TRIBE: One particular piece of advice, though, along a somewhat different dimension: state constitutions, either as written or as construed by state courts, ought not to hitch their wagon too often to the federal constitutional star. There is now a tendency, several years old, to read state constitutions in a way somewhat independent from the federal Constitution. That has been followed by a counter-tendency, in various states, to try to prevent state courts from giving their constitutions a meaning different from the way federal judges construe the analogous federal provision.

But if the states are to serve their optimal function as laboratories in the controversial areas of search and seizure, the death penalty, abortion funding, and the like, we don't want to make them carbon copies of federal law. I would want to resist any expansion of that trend.

LOUIS FISHER, Library of Congress: On the question of how to interpret the Constitution, the panelists spent all their time on how judges go about that task. Professor Tribe, you've talked about method and technique difficulties; Judge Wallace talked about the anxieties of having nine justices do this.

But it's certainly true that Congress and the president have important roles—and I'm not just talking about the initial interpretation, which the Supreme Court would acknowledge. Isn't there a much more dynamic process, a dialogue among all three branches, with the duty to interpret the Constitution placed not just on the Supreme Court or on the judiciary? Don't we have a much more vigorous dialogue among all three branches, and also with the states?

PROFESSOR BERNS: With the increasing emphasis on the Court and with the Court entering areas where, in my judgment, it ought not to enter, officials in other branches of the government tend to think that interpreting the Constitution is none of their business. The most egregious example was the second round of the effort to secure ratification of the so-called Equal Rights Amendment, in which sixty-five senators sponsored that amendment's rebirth or resurrection. Its chief sponsor was Senator Paul Tsongas, of Massachusetts, who made the mistake of testifying before the Senate Judiciary Committee on its behalf. He was asked time and time again: What does this amendment mean? And he answered time and time again: "I don't know. It is up to the courts to say."

Now, this was the chief sponsor of a proposed amendment to the Constitution of the United States, and he believed it was not his job to know what the language meant. That's constitutional irresponsibility.

PROFESSOR TRIBE: I have seen plenty of examples of constitutional irresponsibility, but I would not have used that one. Senator Tsongas was trying to say that no one will know in advance in detail all the applications of a very broad principle, such as the Equal Protection Clause. If we had asked those who wrote the free-speech clause of the First Amendment what its interpretation would be in any half dozen cases before the Ninth Circuit, or the D. C. Circuit, they would have had to say, with humility, "We are really not sure."

But I do agree with the general thrust of Professor Berns's point, and that is, as Professor Fisher's question suggests, we ought not to treat constitutional interpretation as simply a puzzle about constitutional review among the three branches of government. We need a constitutional theory adequate to all three. That's why, in a context as difficult as abortion, it is no answer at all to say courts should have stayed out of it. Even if courts *had* stayed out of it, it would have been, and some day still may be, the responsibility of lawmakers, sworn to uphold the Constitution, to decide themselves whether a particular restriction on abortion does or does not violate a woman's liberty without due process of law.

We need a constitutional theory, in other words, that is not obsessed with the legitimacy of judicial interpretation—that's one issue, but it's not the only issue.

JUDGE MIKVA: If the Congress and the state legislatures had addressed the subject of school segregation or the subject of state legislative malapportionment—much of which existed even under constitutions that specifically required reapportionment—then the Court might have been able to let that cup pass, to everybody's relief. Then we would have had no basis for this program.

The quickest way to empty either chamber of the Congress is to get up and say "I'd like to discuss the constitutionality of this bill." Immediately the members say, "Well, that's for the courts," and go back to their offices.

As someone who believes in the primacy of the first branch of government, I find that very distressing. It dismayed me mightily before, and it still dismays me, that my former congressional colleagues just don't think it's their responsibility to worry about the constitutionality of an issue. Maybe part of the reason is that fewer lawyers are elected to the Congress than before, and—present company excepted—a lot of nonlawyers think it's not their responsibility to worry about the Constitution. Well, I happen to think it is.

DR. GOLDWIN: Well, it's my responsibility to announce that this concludes another Public Policy Forum presented by the American Enterprise Institute for Public Policy Research.

The AEI Project, "A Decade of Study of the Constitution," of which publication of this Public Policy Forum transcript is one activity, has been funded in part by a grant from the National Endowment for the Humanities.